RESILIENT HEART

Transcending the Death of Your Loved One

GAIL SAUNDERS

Praise for Resilient Heart® – Transcending the Death of Your Loved One

"Gail is a trailblazer in the transformation of grief. I've worked with grievers for more than twenty-five years and no one has mourned more creatively, soulfully, and completely. I encouraged her to write a book to inspire others." ~ Marilyn Grosboll, RN, Grief and Self-Esteem Coach, Instructor City College Continuing Education Santa Barbara

"Gail has the ability to express all sides of life and death. Through tears and laughter, her grace, spirituality, and courage shine through. She is quite remarkable in how she grew through her own mourning experience after the death of her beloved husband, Frank. Now she sensitively guides others to do the same. This book is both inspirational and transformational." ~ Russell L. McIntyre, Th.D., Professor of Medical Ethics and Health Law, Robert Wood Johnson Medical School, Rutgers, The State University of New Jersey, Ordained Lutheran Clergyman

"As a Funeral Celebrant I witness much grief, but also much glory. This topic is so profound and needed. Saunders offers so much of her heart along with inspiration and good sound advice. I am sure that *Resilient Heart* will be very helpful to folks in mourning." ~ Donna Henes, Urban Shaman and author of *Celestial Auspicious Occasions*

Published by: www.TransformationBooks.com

ISBN: 978-0-9862901-1-4
Library of Congress Control No: 2014960169

Cover design by Gail Saunders and Ranilo Cabo
Layout and typesetting by Ranilo Cabo
Editor: Marlene Oulton, www.MarleneOulton.com
Proofreader: Corinne Dixon, www.CorinneDixon.com
Interior artwork created by: Gail Saunders
Interior photograph: Martin Prentice
Author photograph: H. Gunzelmann
Printed in the United States of America

Grateful acknowledgment is made to the following for permission to reprint previously published material: Donna Henes, excerpt from her book *Celestially Auspicious Occasions* MONARCH PRESS (1996); *Seasons, Cycles and Celebrations,* Rashani Réa for her poem *The Unbroken* from her book *Beyond Brokenness,* XLIBRIS, CORP. (2009); Kimberly Marooney for excerpt from her book *Angel Blessings: Cards of Sacred Guidance and Inspiration,* FAIR WINDS PRESS (2010), and Katherine Rosengren for her untitled poem.

A portion of the proceeds from the sale of this book will be donated to causes the publisher supports.

This book is dedicated to my beloved Frank, the catalyst for this book, whose heart was huge. Our love will always be a gift.

For Marilyn, a loving friend and guide through my grief journey after Frank died. Just as Frank died of cancer, so did she a few years later.

I miss you both… still.

Acknowledgments

MY BELOVED FRANK CONTINUES to expand my heart with his immense love. He made me promise his death would help others. That vow was the catalyst that paved the way to this book *Resilient Heart*®, and to my own heart healing.

I thank my sister, Velvet Hammond, for being my rock and best friend. Her unwavering encouragement and love supported me during my *Resilient Heart*® Journey after Frank died, during the writing of this book, and I know will always bless me.

I am grateful to my small but dynamic family for always being there for me with so much love and joy: Chad, Brittney, Waverly, and Anika.

Marilyn Grosboll was a priceless mentor during my mourning with her course *Growing Through Loss* which I took for five semesters. She was such a compassionate and wise guide and friend.

Roseanne Tillotson blesses my life with her amazing friendship and I appreciate her many hours of skill and love in the preliminary editing of this manuscript. I'm sure at times she had a tough job cleaning up my act.

Susana Wahl and Brian Kovac graciously did the first proofreading of this manuscript and I appreciate their keen eyesight and insight.

I am indebted to other friends who have believed in me and my message and have enthusiastically cheered me on to get this book out into the world. There are too many to list, but I want to specifically acknowledge Helen and Peter Preston, Clare and Martin Prentice, Rose and Liz Blancpain, Chris and Russ McIntyre, and Stephen Hennessey.

All the hospice patients and their families I worked with through the years, as well as my fellow grievers who have deeply influenced and inspired *Resilient Heart*®, I thank you.

Thank you to Christine Kloser who helped develop this baby with her incredible teachings and motivation that she provides for transformational authors.

I gratefully acknowledge Marlene Oulton for her magical skill, insight, and sensitivity as my editor. She was an absolute delight to work with.

Gratitude to Corinne Dixon for her proofreading abilities and joining my team with such enthusiasm.

I was blessed to have Carrie Jareed as my midwife in the unfolding publishing process of Resilient Heart.

My heart is filled with gratitude to my Divine Source for constantly being by my side, even in the darkest moments of my grief and guiding me to what I call mourning light.

CONTENTS

Introduction

DEATH STRIKES LIKE A VIOLENT TORNADO, shattering your life with cruel abandon and leaving it unrecognizable. In the wake of its destruction you are left disoriented. You have been catapulted into grief. You feel anything but resilient and invincible. Widow… orphan… mourning… abandonment – all concepts and titles you never associated with yourself. I want you to know that you can rise from the rubble of your loss. Your heart and true nature are resilient, and your spirit is invincible. Let's look at resilience. It is the ability to recover and survive from the intense shock and disbelief after the death of a loved one. It is the ability to integrate such a loss into your psyche and your life. Resilience is being capable of transforming feelings of being broken into breakthroughs which lead to inner strength and experiencing renewed hope. It is the ability to carry on.

By being conscious and constructive in the mourning state you can connect to these qualities and integrate, heal, and transcend the death of your loved one. Resilient Heart® will coach you through your mourning process. With compassionate guidance you will learn how to navigate grief with knowledge and creative tools. You will be assisted in alleviating the pain of your amplified emotions and difficult thoughts. Your actions will empower you as you heal by expressing your loss and honoring your loved one.

This book is not only about death, but also about living. You can live after great loss. If you are in the first phase of grief, the thought of living without your loved one seems unattainable right now and perhaps not even desired. However, you can learn to live wholeheartedly, not merely go through the motions. At this devastating time there is also an opportunity for tremendous transformation through self-discovery.

My mission with this book is to ignite your inner strength, courage, heart, and wisdom. I aim to assist you to reconnect to your resilience during your time of mourning and transition so that you, too, will continue your life with passion. I have a lot of experience with death and loss. The death of my beloved husband Frank pulled me into an abyss of grief, but with hard work I emerged on the other side stronger, wiser, and once again glad to be alive. I have also experienced the loss of my parents, friends, pets, and also the deaths of my patients during the six years I volunteered with Hospice of Santa Barbara. I encouraged my patients to live their passion until their last breath. After the death of a patient, I assisted their grieving families with their healing process. I will guide you to take control at a time when everything feels out of your control. Believe it or not, you *can* orchestrate how you mourn.

When my Frank died of lung cancer, I promised him that I would write this book to help others navigate through this strange labyrinth of mourning. I also made the same commitment to Marilyn Grosboll who was a wonderful mentor during my grief. Marilyn told me that I mourned more fully and creatively than any mourner she had worked with in twenty-five years as a grief coach, and she encouraged me to write this book. She even pulled out her wallet and paid for the first copy before it was published!

The path of grief is not one that we choose or want. However, loss is a universal experience and it is a rare being who is left unscathed. Common as it is, when it happens to us, we feel alone and lost. Please recognize that you are not alone. Help is available as you struggle to process your loss. Integration of the death of your loved one will lead to healing, even if that seems unbelievable right now. It does not matter where you are in the process of dealing with your loss; this book will speak to you and offer solace, as well as encourage you to fully engage in your mourning process. You've already begun to take control by reaching for this book.

In the North American culture, we are often very segregated from death so that when you face it head-on you don't have others' experiences to lean on. My hope is that in sharing some of my experiences of grief and those of others, I can aid you on your path. I will both comfort you and challenge you to take actions to mourn consciously as we wade through the wilderness of grief together. By consciously mourning, I mean to choose constructive and healthy ways to cope with the affront to your being that death has wrought.

Mourning is a journey of the heart and soul, an outward expression of the internal grief caused by the death of your loved one. The profound pain you are feeling is a testament to the love you have for your loved one. If you love, there will be grief with loss. Renewal can happen when you allow light to shine into the cracks of your exploded heart. Persevere with your grief process.

If you try to repress grief or internalize it the suffering increases. **Grief doesn't have a shelf life.** It has all the patience in the world and it will sit and fester until you process it. A high percentage of grievers become ill within a year of loss. They freeze the pain and emotions in their bodies and minds rather than dealing with them. Throughout this book I will give you many suggestions of how to express and process your feelings and turbulent thoughts. Taking actions where possible is important when you are feeling so much is out of your control right now.

You have experienced a life-altering event, and your total being – physical, mental, emotional, and spiritual – needs to recalibrate. Your loss needs to be acknowledged, honored, and integrated into your life. This doesn't happen overnight and it is not an easy process. Please be patient with yourself there are skills you can learn. You can do this!

Each griever has their own unique process, but there are many similar experiences and feelings along the road. Learning how other mourners have dealt with aspects of their grief can help you find your right path. There are common stepping stones, arranged perhaps in a different order than the ones I took, to cross the raging river of grief on the way to resilience and even transcendence. With awareness choose your steps, making them wise ones.

Throughout the book I use several names such as God, Spirit, and the Divine. I am speaking of the powerful force of unconditional love, Divine intelligence and creation which sustains all life. If I use any name that doesn't resonate with you, please substitute whatever term feels right and comfortable for you.

I have organized this book around subjects that you can turn to as they fit your experience, interest, or need. During my bereavement I kept journals of my emotions, thoughts, and experiences. I have interspersed excerpts from my entries throughout the book and have drawn on my hospice experiences as well. I think it is important not only to read about grief, but also express it. I suggest possible activities in the **Heartfelt Suggestions** section in each chapter. I also invite you to my website GailSaunders.com to receive the free *Resilient Heart*® Workbook where you can write your responses and insights. I am encouraging you to make this an interactive and creative experience. These suggestions are meant to encourage and invite you to engage consciously in your grief process. You need not do all that are suggested. Remember to do this sacred work at your own pace.

By experiencing my grief fully, I have been shown that **love never dies.** There are no boundaries with the experience called death. I thought I understood this before Frank's passing, but was given proof afterward that the spirit continues to exist on another plane.

As a loved one dies, those remaining are born into a new and different life. It isn't a chosen birth, but rather a rebirth of you. The pain of rebirth eventually recedes like the tides; not suddenly, more like as night melts into dawn. Transformation and personal growth finally came out of my chaos. You too, are greater than your grief. With hope and conscious mourning you can transcend the death of your loved one.

Hold fast to your *Resilient Heart*® and begin your journey. I light a candle to brighten your way when the darkness is unbearable. Thank you for the privilege of walking with you on your *Resilient Heart*® Journey. I hope with all my heart that this book will help you on your courageous path to gaining greater strength, self-knowledge, and resilience.

"Man never made any material as resilient as the human spirit." ~
Bern Williams

CHAPTER ONE

REPERCUSSIONS: Champagne and Ashes

"IS THIS SERIOUS?" the voice on the phone asked.

I repeated that my husband had just died and yes, I considered that very serious.

"But is it an emergency?" she then asked dryly.

"Yes, to me it is an emergency," I declared in disbelief.

She continued to question, "But are you in a state where you could hurt yourself or another?"

Emphatically, I said, "No!" However, I thought that I was going to hurt her if she didn't give me this clearance. I pondered if I hadn't needed counseling before I called her, I surely did now! I was calling to get the necessary okay from my health provider for a few visits with a therapist and finally was successful.

Looking back on the first months after my life was changed forever I would call this phase of my mourning process "Champagne and Ashes." My life and my husband were in ashes. It was also a time to celebrate Frank and the amazing love relationship I had been blessed to share with him.

Shock and Disbelief

The tapestry of your life has been slashed by death; you are unraveling. Shock and disbelief are common feelings. The magnitude of the loss and its repercussions are just too immense to absorb, the pain too enormous to process. Thus, you close down for protection. Luckily, during the time immediately after your loss you are usually surrounded by family and friends. They can direct you as to what must be done to handle the essentials of death, like dealing with a mortuary and planning a ceremony. Everything seems so surreal. You feel as though you are in a bubble watching others carrying on with their lives as if nothing had happened, while your life as you knew it is gone.

I was depleted from the 24-hour care I had gladly provided for Frank for four months. I consider there is no greater honor or privilege than to help a loved one die with as much grace and dignity as possible, sharing those difficult yet precious last few months. My focus had been completely on him 24/7, and I had been so strong handling his care. But my emotions had exhausted me and I fell apart after he died. Fortunately, my sister Velvet came to California to support me a few days before Frank died and stayed for the week afterward. Frank and I had moved to Santa Cruz just four months before his death and were there only one day when his symptoms erupted on Christmas morning. For the next four months, the only people I knew or saw were in the medical profession, as that became our complete world.

We were in a wonderful hospital in Santa Cruz that permitted me to spend all the time I wanted with Frank as he was dying. The nurses had been trained in Reiki energy work by the hospital, and since I am also a Reiki Master/Teacher, I found that comforting. Reiki is a beautiful way to attune someone to balance and peace. We were also blessed to have Barbara, an incredible harpist, play her music in his room as he was leaving his body. As soon as Frank died or birthed into spirit, I anointed his body with rose oil and waited until all of his energy had left his body which took four hours. Walking out of that room and leaving Frank was one of the most difficult things I have ever done. I went directly to the hospital chapel and wailed. Then Velvet and I began the important focus of celebrating Frank's amazing spirit. He was a big man, 6 feet 6-inches tall, with broad shoulders, but his spirit was even larger than his frame. We bought champagne and balloons, and that night at home we went onto the deck and let the balloons soar into the stars, then popped the champagne. Through torrential tears, we drank to my husband's unforgettable spirit. I let a few friends know of his death and they called others. At my suggestion, loved ones released balloons all around the world that night. I made sure they knew to use only biodegradable balloons with no strings that could hurt birds. Friends later shared that it was perfect since it also gave them something to do when they heard the news.

The next day we had to visit the crematorium. That was a smack of reality. When Frank died I had credit card bills of $37,000. There was no life insurance and I hadn't worked since his illness surfaced. For financial reasons I opted to bypass a mortuary service. This was a case of you-get-what-you-pay-for. Any sense of courtesy or compassion was non-existent. I hope your experience is, or was, much better.

If you find that black humor or seeing the humorous side to your tragic event comes to the surface, don't be surprised. Just like the shock, the humor is a way for you to cope. Allow it to flow. I sure did. It began on the way to the crematorium.

Velvet was driving and all of a sudden a whole joke came to me, unusual because I would normally start telling one and need Frank to remind me of the punch line. I shared with Velvet that this was either the perfect joke or the most inappropriate one. She wanted to hear it anyway. Here goes: *A woman's husband died and she had him cremated. She brought his ashes home and poured them on the table. She began playing with the ashes. She said, "Tom, remember that fur coat I always wanted and you wouldn't buy one for me? I bought one today." She continued to play with his ashes. "Oh, Tom, also that holiday I wanted to take to Spain for years and you wouldn't even look at the brochures? I have tickets to leave tomorrow. Oh, and Tom, remember that blow job you always wanted?" With great gusto she blew the ashes all over the room.* Velvet nearly had a wreck! We felt Frank's presence there. I knew he was whispering the joke in my ear and telling me to lighten up!

At the crematorium the man who worked with us was quite unfeeling, never even acknowledging my loss. After reading more about cremation from a brochure than I ever wanted to know, he asked if I had any questions. I asked what the cost would be as I was financially strapped. He quoted a price that shocked me. I told him that my mother had died and her cremation had been only a third of his quote. He very sarcastically asked in what state she had died. When I told him Texas, he said in a superior tone, "Well, *this* is California." I turned to my sister and suggested that we get an ice cream truck and take Frank to Texas. The man squawked, "That is against the law!" Then I looked at the cost of moving Frank from the hospital to the crematorium. That, too, was outrageous as the hospital was merely across the street. I said it would be cheaper to rent a limo with champagne and bring him in style. The man didn't laugh, but it made me feel better. I have spoken to others in the throes of loss, and found that black humor is not at all unusual; it can be a safety valve to help you get through an unbearable situation. You aren't being disrespectful of your lost one. I'm sure Frank was cheering me on from above.

When I started writing this book, I asked my sister and some good friends to give me feedback. I could not remember those initial weeks after Frank died. The entire period is a blur to me. I do recall feeling that I was just going through the motions of living, rather like a zombie. Velvet recalls that I was nonfunctional; I couldn't even write a check correctly. I was fragile, emotionally wrecked, stunned, paralyzed, overwhelmed, devastated, and brought to my knees. I was yearning for my past, and I was angry. She also remembers that I was waiting at a bus stop and someone came up to me and tried to give me some money because I looked so low-down.

In Greece, people wear black armbands to let others know they are grieving. In our culture people don't have a clue how fragile you are or why. That reminds me of a time just before Frank died. I was in the grocery store and the porcelain angel pin I had worn every day fell off my blouse and shattered on the floor. We had just heard how much worse Frank's condition was: now there were at least six brain tumors and more growths in his bones. Immediately, I was on all fours sobbing and hunting for every piece of my angel. It was imperative that I find every shard. All of a sudden I realized people were taking a wide detour around me and looking at me strangely. I thought, "They think I've lost it! Well, you have, Gail, and rightfully so. Carry on!"

I became very direct in those first weeks. The day Frank died a cashier asked how my day was going and I said, "Terrible, my husband just died!"

Velvet gasped, "She won't ask anyone else how they are." I just couldn't say fine when nothing was fine. I had to be authentic! During this initial time of loss, all in all I was quite charming to be around, I'm sure. But let me reassure you that all of these behaviors are normal. Please don't judge yourself.

I knew I needed counseling. I think each of us at some time in our life needs assistance to cope with major events. I had to overcome some programming from my father who said that only someone who belonged in a mental hospital needed help. I knew if there was ever a time I needed therapy, this was it. During Frank's last month of life the wonderful oncologist we visited insisted that all his patients and their spouses receive counseling. Unfortunately, we had only two sessions before Frank died. I wanted to continue with the same therapist and was able to get the necessary clearance for a couple more sessions. Be open to therapy if you feel it can help right now.

Mindless

For months I felt like I didn't have a mind. It seemed like I had a concussion or was in a coma. I didn't realize my brain lived in Frank's body. I repeatedly did mindless acts. I locked my keys in the car three times. Not only did I lock them in the car, I also left the car running.

The most embarrassing episode was when I was looking for Frank's will. I found a locked metal box and thought "Eureka! This is it!" I hauled it to the locksmith. Three men attacked the box and it finally sprang open. A pile of photos cascaded onto the table. In horror, I realized the photos were all racy ones that Frank had taken of me several years back. I scooped them into my purse as quickly as I could, wanting just to pay and get out of there. Then I realized I had left my wallet on the seat in my unlocked car. To my chagrin, I had to walk out to the car and return to pay.

It took me nine months to find that will.

I moved back to Santa Barbara four months after Frank died. The first morning I woke up in my new apartment I thought my car had been stolen. I called the police and learned that it had been towed; I had blocked someone's driveway. I thought I was losing my mind, but in a grief group one woman shared that she had forgotten to push the button on her garage door opener and drove her car through the door. Many of us shared that we weren't present. We were thinking of our loss or floating in another world beside ourselves.

Despair

Physical Repercussions

I had horrible nightmares about the crematorium and death as I waited that first week to hear when I could bring Frank's ashes home. I will address dreams in Chapter 3. Unusual dreams are normal as you adjust to your new situation. It is also common to repeatedly have flashbacks to the death. So awake or asleep, you live in what used to be only a nightmare. My sleep was very disturbed. For the four months of Frank's illness I had to set the alarm nearly every hour to give him some sort of medication during the night. Now, although I was exhausted, sleep was so elusive.

Physical sensations were intense after my loss. It felt as though there was a large lump in my throat, accompanied by searing pain and extreme heat in my heart center. I asked Velvet to touch the area of my heart, and she could feel it, too: like a hot iron was burning in the center of my chest. For a year after our mother died we both felt as though there was an actual hole in the center of our chests. All these sensations were repercussions from our wounded hearts. I kept catching myself sitting and rocking without a rocking chair, a self-soothing technique as Velvet, who is a counselor, explained. That continued for quite a while.

Repeatedly I found myself holding my breath or only taking shallow quick breaths. I have taught techniques to help alleviate stress for over forty years yet I wasn't practicing them. One signal of stress is the type of breathing I just described. I know that if one changes their breathing to a slow and deep cleansing breath, peace will follow. When I finally realized how I was breathing I would put my hand over my broken heart and breathe in slowly and deeply. Concentrating on my breath was a lifeline to a semblance of balance and peace.

I also cried incessantly. I wished I owned stock in a tissue company as I would have been rich from the way I was going through boxes and boxes of them! By the way, crying is covered in Chapter 4 and truly is a part of healing.

Handling Necessities

It is sad that you have to make so many decisions and do such important things when you are in this state. I was told to fill out reams of forms for Frank's job, even though I wouldn't receive any money since he hadn't worked there long enough for even a sick day. Due to the high cost of rent, I had to get out of the large home we had just rented or get roommates. Should I move back to Santa Barbara, where I had friends and had a practice before I left? I had to go through all our belongings that had been in storage for seventeen years, during which time we had traveled and lived on a Greek island for nearly ten years. We had brought these boxes to California just as the illness surfaced and they hadn't been opened in all those years. Once I decided to move back to Santa Barbara I had to downsize to a one-bedroom apartment. What to do with all these things? My wonderful nephew Chad came to help with a huge estate auction. It was all such a nightmare. I knew the grief books recommend not moving, but it would have been more difficult for me to stay in a new community where I didn't have friends, and I desperately needed my friends. I didn't have the energy to go out and meet new people. Your situation is unique and you make the best decisions possible at the time with the knowledge you have and the state you are in. I finally learned not to expect of myself what I normally would or could do under more normal circumstances.

This is the time to let others help you! It is important to make things as easy as possible for yourself right now. Velvet made a list of things that others could do for me when they called and asked how they could help. It's difficult to think straight when asked, and most people will respond with, "Oh, there's nothing you can do." Now I had a list to refer to. One of the things on my list was to get a massage. When Bob, a dear friend of ours called and asked what he could do, I said I needed to be touched. Before I could add that a professional massage would be wonderful, Bob quickly said he couldn't do anything like that! We both ended up laughing.

If you have the resources to hire a lawyer, they can be of tremendous help. Frank, who had been a lawyer, was just fifty-one when he died, and we never gave a thought that death could happen so soon. Because of the brain tumors he couldn't focus, couldn't help me with the many crucial decisions to be made. I didn't know where any of the important papers were; I didn't even know the password to our computer! And I didn't have the funds to hire an attorney. I now recommend to all couples that they make sure each knows where all significant documents are kept. I also suggest they exchange roles for several months in order to teach each other the different responsibilities each person handles while there is no emotional pressure. For example, if one pays the bills, teach the system to the other. I also put forward the idea to tell each other daily what they appreciate about the other. Frank and I did do the latter, but had we incorporated the other two suggestions, it would have made my journey so much easier.

Honoring Your Loved One

This first phase of my grief also consisted of celebration. Having some sort of ceremony helps you begin to integrate the loss into your psyche. I wanted to celebrate the wonderful man who I was blessed to have had in my life for thirty-three years. I planned two gatherings to honor Frank. One was in Santa Barbara where we had recently lived and had friends. I was fortunate to get the last available booking in a park on the exact day I wanted. Velvet and I had written the ceremony the week after Frank died; however, I was in no shape to officiate, so my good friend Sharon, who is also an ordained minister, conducted the service. Afterward, we released over one hundred white balloons. I organized another service in Texas where both our families lived. This service was held at my sister's church and her minister wove my words into the ceremony. I had Frank's brother bring fresh pine boughs from trees Frank and his father had planted when he was a small boy. I was careful of who I invited. I didn't want anything to upset me any more than I already was. I recalled how chaotic things were with Frank's dad's funeral. These turning points in our lives can bring out the best and the worst in people. There is a very interesting book inside me waiting to be written about that funeral! I was in a mode of self-preservation when Frank died and I did protect myself. I have never felt so vulnerable in my life.

Looking back on those first few months after my loss, I realize that I experienced all the stages of grief in a blender. I felt so much anger. I was angry that Frank died and I was alone. I was angry at the medical establishment. I was shocked and furious when two men who had been friends of ours came on to me within weeks of Frank's death. One suggested I come live with him, that he would be "sensitive" and wouldn't expect sex immediately! Oh, yes, very sensitive. The other, who with his wife, had come to one of the celebrations I held for Frank, said he was always attracted to me but didn't tell me because he felt it was inappropriate while Frank was living. He said that he felt it was appropriate now to tell me how he felt and asked when we could get together. I told him that it was totally inappropriate and to never contact me again. I suppose I could thank both men for giving me an outlet for my anger. Refer to Chapter 4 for more on anger.

The beginning of grief reminds me of something my friend Susana says. When she is experiencing something she would rather not be living she says, "Not my movie." All the strange and intense emotions and bizarre experiences during the grieving process are not your movie.

Heartfelt Suggestions ∽♡∾

Now it is time to go to a quiet place where you can take some time for yourself. Bring a notebook and pen.

1. **Breathe.** Put your hand on your heart and close your eyes. Become aware of your body and choose to let it relax. Drop your shoulders. Breathe in as slowly and deeply as possible and try to match the length of your inhale and exhale. Think of breathing peace into your broken heart. As you exhale think of releasing the pain. With each breath allow your body to melt a little more. Let go.

2. **Stabilize.** Stand or sit with your feet apart, creating a firm stance. Imagine breathing balance from the earth up through your left foot. Let it come up to your heart and

then exhale down your right side and direct your breath out through the right foot and back into the earth with your thought. Hold the intention that your exhale carries away anything that is keeping you from being in balance at this moment. Repeat this for several breaths.

Now open your eyes and begin reading and reflect on the suggestions. This is part of your conscious mourning and it is sacred work.

1. Are you sharing your story with someone? This facilitates your healing process, even if it is writing it in a notebook just for you to read.

2. Are you experiencing any secondary losses, for example, loss of home or financial security, due to the death of your loved one?

3. Are you accepting and seeking support from family, friends, and professionals such as a lawyer, accountant, and perhaps a counselor and/or a spiritual adviser? Make a list of how someone can help you now.

4. Are there any things you can do to protect yourself while feeling so vulnerable? Perhaps you may not take a call immediately, allowing you to handle things when you are up to it. I avoided crowds for a long time as it felt like too much stimulus. I turned down invitations if being alone seemed more appropriate at the time.

5. How can you celebrate and honor your loved one?

6. What physical repercussions of grief are you experiencing? If any of your symptoms persist, I suggest you check with your physician to make sure that your own health is on track. I also feel that writing about your feelings in a notebook or journal is also beneficial. You're letting your hurt and grief out of your body via the written word.

7. What makes you feel loved and alive? Please do something kind for yourself during this period. Have you considered having a massage?

CHAPTER TWO

REALIZATION: Dancing in the Dark

YOU ARE NOW AT A PLACE WHERE the initial shock is wearing off and stark reality sets in. As you emerge from the fog, your emotions are all over the map because life as you knew it has irreversibly changed. You have been forced to begin the Journey of Grief.

What is Grief?

Grief is the normal process of reacting after loss. I reiterate that it is a natural human response and can be multi-faceted in nature: physical, emotional, behavioral, mental, social, spiritual, or all of these emotions. You can grieve many different kinds of experiences, not just the death of a loved one: divorce or relationship breakup, loss of a job, loss of your health or that of someone close to you, a move, the loss of a dear pet, or loss of independence at old age. Whenever there is change there is a loss of what was. The only constant in life is change, so it is something we all face, and depending on the importance of the loss you've encountered, the magnitude of the grief that follows will be proportional. If you are reading this book I know you have experienced the painful death of your loved one. Your grief is very deep with major repercussions. I am so sorry for the personal loss that has forced you onto your *Resilient Heart*® Journey.

Disorientation is one of the common aspects of deep grief because you are in unfamiliar territory. This major loss must be integrated into your life, and it will take a while to craft the next chapter of your life without your loved one.

Disengaging from normal activities is another common occurrence. I call this "cocooning." It is quite normal (because you feel raw and vulnerable) to protect yourself and allow for healing, much as you would place a bandage over a wound to protect it until the skin heals itself. During the period of deep grief after my husband died I didn't become a hermit, but I attempted to create a balance between time with me and time with others. I didn't even recognize myself. I had been a part of "we" for so long that I had to excavate my life and find "me" again. At times it felt like a tedious archeological dig. Your connections to others make up a part of your identity and as you assimilate this heartbreaking loss you are redefining who you are. Grief is an inward and outward process. The inside job is one that you need to do alone.

Disillusionment is also a normal reaction that can surface after the death of a loved one or after any profound loss. Many dreams and values are shattered when someone you love dies, and perhaps you are left feeling disenchanted with life. It is easy to wonder if your life has purpose. When you no longer have order in your world it is easy to question your faith. Nothing makes sense.

I want you to hear that what you are experiencing, although unique to you, is not unusual with a major loss. Give yourself permission to be right where you are even though it is very uncomfortable at this moment. Hold yourself in compassion and understanding as you begin to integrate the death of your loved one into your life as it is now.

People die in different ways. Your loved one might have died after a major illness, as my Frank did, within three months of his diagnosis. Your loved one's health might have deteriorated over a much longer period and you had to witness that suffering for an unbearable length of time. Your beloved might have died suddenly by accident or murder. You might be reconciling the suicide of your loved one. I lost my partner where you might have lost your child, a parent, sibling, or dear friend. You might be dealing with multiple deaths, perhaps from a car accident in which you might have even been the driver. Each kind of tragic loss has different elements as well as many similar traits.

When an illness is prolonged for months or even years with death being a certainty, the grief process has begun long before death occurs. This is called **anticipatory grief**. When Frank's symptoms exploded to the surface on that Christmas Day, my grieving began. He and I could no longer share physical lovemaking, and due to the brain tumors, we couldn't hold the deep and interesting conversations that we had always relished. On the other hand, we could say the important things to each other as well as say good-bye during those few months. I didn't have time to ponder my grief with each loss: every moment was spent caring for Frank's needs and making him as comfortable and happy as I knew how. I watched his strong body deteriorate before my eyes and finally knew he had to leave that body; it could no longer sustain him.

Often, with an extended illness, there is a wish for it all just to end. That was Frank's biggest fear: that I would get so tired of the situation and just want it to be over. Many who have been close to those who are dying have had such thoughts and then felt tremendous guilt when the person did finally die. If you have silently wished for the end of your loved one's suffering, please know it is normal and try not to judge yourself.

If your dear one died suddenly, you had no pre-grieving period to help you begin to adjust. This lack of transition time makes the event feel even more surreal. It could have been a violent ending, leaving you filled with rage and thoughts of revenge, or it's left you with survivor's guilt. You might not have had the opportunity to say goodbye. Again, what you are feeling is natural; allow your emotions to flow. We will talk much more about this in Chapter 4 where I suggest how to cope in constructive ways with your kaleidoscope of feelings and wild thoughts.

The circumstances of your loss are unique and personal as well as devastating. Needing to share your story is quite prevalent and it is good to relate it. The telling assists you in beginning to accept the truth of loss; it is beneficial to express the pain and begin to release it. You are beginning to give voice to your anguish, to mourn the emotions of grief. Your story is too immense to stifle.

There is another common reaction when loss cracks you open: past losses can resurface, especially if they weren't processed completely. I presumed that I had dealt many years before with the reality that I couldn't have children; however, when I heard other grievers repeatedly talk about the solace they had with their children after a death of a loved one, I felt like I was being stabbed in the heart. So on top of the current pain, there was definitely residual grief that still needed to be processed. I longed for the comfort and wisdom of my mother when Frank died, but she had passed eight years before. Her loss was highlighted again. You, too, might be experiencing grief from your past welling up to the surface.

You might have experienced several deep losses within a short period. I recently spoke with a woman who lost three loved ones within a year. Multiple deaths or other major losses can compound your grief process.

One major loss can impact several areas of your life. When Frank died, I lost the place where we had been living, most of my belongings, my financial security, and a few friends. You might feel deserted by specific individuals. There can be a lack of support from someone who you thought would be there for you, but isn't forthcoming. A few months after I moved back to Santa Barbara, I attended a day workshop presented by Deborah Levinson, a clinical social worker. She gave a list of characteristics that are thought to be significant for adjustment to loss of a spouse. I think they work for other relationships as well. The main ones were age, health, how the person died, support systems, other roles, and resilience ability. In my past I was able to bounce back after other losses, but the adjustment to Frank's death was on another scale. This loss dwarfed any other loss I had ever encountered. I learned at the age of fifty-one that I was considered a young widow, the category applying to anyone younger than fifty-six. I have always hated the word *widow*. It feels strange in my mouth. I looked it up in a word-origin book: it means loss of oneself. I hated the word even more. I didn't lose *me*; I lost my husband! But for many months I did wonder where the confident and capable woman I had considered to be *me* had gone. Six months after my husband's death I attended my first public gathering, a Halloween costume party. I decided to go as myself since I hadn't seen me in awhile!

Transition is the state you are in, and the challenge is to embrace rather than resist the forced change. A forced transition is much more difficult than one you would freely choose. Change is inevitable, but we can create or co-create some of the aspects. I knew these things; I had even taught them, but I had to be reminded of them while I was grieving. I began to take some control when possible and I began to feel less vulnerable and more powerful. Marilyn Grosboll, an incredible teacher whose course, *Growing Through Loss*, I attended in Santa Barbara, struck a chord with me when she said that the pain of change is temporary, but the pain of not changing is permanent.

Most major adjustments in life are punctuated with the state of limbo for a period of time. This can be confusing and chaotic. I have personally defined security as having the ability to adjust to change with as much grace as possible. I had been in that place of transition many times, but nothing compared to this. When a situation in life shifts as dramatically as with a death, there is a tendency for the perceptual markers in your life to alter or disappear. The rug has been pulled out from under you. I wondered if I would ever feel stability again or even find one sure foothold. Not only did I not have a foothold, I often felt like an acrobat that had let go of one swing and was soaring unsupported through the void of the unknown with no other swing in sight. It is scary and there is risk. It takes faith. Where is the next swing and where will it take you? In her book, *Celestially Auspicious Occasions: Seasons, Cycles and Celebrations,* Donna Henes, a ceremonial artist and urban shaman, shared these poignant thoughts on being in the void:

"The terror is the turning point, the time for determination. It is at this critical moment that we can consciously choose to dwell in the dark for a while longer – for as long as it takes – *despite* our fear. We can decide to take it on and take it in. To deal with it. To go where it takes us. To explore the blind byways of our pain, inching along, feeling our way with our tongues if we have to. To plumb our emotional depths and mine that precious secret ore of our own heartfelt experience. To feel our heart actually break, explode apart, like a geode, revealing the glittering crystals growing inside. To engage passionately in all that life has to offer."

I have come to think of this period as a time of dancing in the dark. It is a time when your ego can't control the huge impact of your loss and loses its grip. However, with time your *Resilient Heart*® begins to open, and slowly inner wisdom and guidance begin to shine through. I had to surrender to the abyss without resistance. It is very difficult to become comfortable with uncertainty, but resisting only compounds the anguish.

Fighting to control that which is uncontrollable is futile and exhausting. Acceptance is called for, although that is usually a gradual shift. A key step toward resilience is acceptance. Liking something is not a requirement for acceptance. I will never like the fact that Frank died, but I have grown to accept the truth that he is no longer here with me in the same way. I wrote in my journal during my mourning:

> *I'm playing with the concept of darkness and light. Mourning light, is it possible? I think giving myself time in the darkness of grief I will be led to light. Maybe I could be led at least to a lighter sense of being than I am experiencing now. Morning light is after the darkness of night. Perhaps there is mourning light after the darkness of loss. I am doodling images to represent dealing with the darkness of the void. Art is helping me express my current thoughts and emotions. The void, the nocturnal abode, the prenatal darkness; it is a diving into the unknown. I call this dancing in the dark, the primordial chaos. I choose to*

dance with the situation rather than resist. I find only more pain when I resist and fight against what is. The darkness is filled with mystery and potential. I choose to dive into the mystery and the possibility. Some of my images are a person diving into a black chaotic shape, a sea of darkness. The black enchantment precedes rebirth, initiation, and enlightenment. Another image is a person dancing alone in the darkness in the shape of the vesica picis which is similar to the shape of an eye. In sacred geometry it is often used with reference to Christ. It is also the shape of the vulva, the doorway of new life. For years I have enjoyed studying symbols and sacred geometry. The potentiality is the germ of all creation, primordial matriarchal, the mystery of being, the beginning, and the womb. Darkness is the ground of the light which emerges from it. It is unmanifested light. It represents transition, where I am. I think of dancing as cosmic creative energy. It is a form of transformation with grace to me. To represent faith I am sketching sprouting seeds and the seed is a vesica picis. I found this quote by author and radio host Cynthia Occelli that explains it beautifully: 'For a seed to achieve its greatest expression, it must come completely undone, the shell cracks, its insides come out and everything changes. To someone who doesn't understand growth, it would look like complete destruction.' When I choose to think of this time of chaos in a more positive light I feel more lightness of being. My sense of hope expands.

I know for a seed to germinate it needs to first be in the darkness of the soil. I wondered what I would germinate into after this heavy weight of dark grief lifted, so I got out *The Book of Runes* by Ralph H. Blum to do a reading. I randomly chose the blank rune which represents the unknowable. The description mirrored what I had been thinking: that it was a time to relinquish control although my greatest fears might surface. It was a time for faith to be tested, and willingness and allowing to be embraced. It ended saying that our challenges can become doorways to new beginnings.

I would rather have kept my past and I had no idea how I could get beyond my pain, but I pondered these wise words. I decided to hold the intention of honoring my dark night of the soul. I chose to plant the seeds that this huge life transition could be an opportunity for transformation and growth.

Facing my pain and not thinking of getting beyond it too quickly seemed the wise goal. The warrior goes to the depth of the well of grief and returns with compassion, according to Mathew Fox in his book *One River, Many Wells*. I held to the hope that guidance was possible even in the dark well of grief. I often felt guided to a book, the words of a song or seeing or hearing what I needed at the time. So I chose not to resist the darkness but rather to dance in it.

As I wondered how long I would be in this intense blackness or if it would ever truly end, my dear friend Roseanne sent me the following poem. It was printed in a magazine and she has carried it in her wallet for over forty years. Reading it gave me renewed hope that this black hole also contained a richness and sacredness if I surrendered to it.

Recovery
The time must come
When all things black
Give in to tones of grey;
When piercing darkness
Of the night
Breaks with the light of day.
It will not happen quickly,
As a wave upon the shore:
Flowing forth, then receding,
Gone forevermore.
But rather, fading slowly
As a mountain turns to plain,
Washed away to nothingness
By gentle drops of rain.
~ Elinor M. Carey

It takes time for reorganization and balance to occur; navigating through the change can be very difficult and at times seem impossible. It is normal to feel adrift with the loss of such an important anchor in your life. Grief can't be rushed. If you cut an emerging butterfly from its cocoon it won't develop properly and be able to fly. The struggle required for it to break through slowly is nature's way of forcing needed fluid from the body to its wings so that it is prepared for flight upon breaking free from its restraints. Soon after Frank died I read a book that said when polled, the average person believed it would take two weeks to grieve the loss of a loved one! I kept rereading that statement; it just didn't compute. I was still numb more than two weeks after Frank died. Be patient with yourself. This is a huge process to forge through this uncharted territory. **Take it one day at**

a time, one step at a time. In the beginning I had to focus on one *minute* at a time. Some days it felt like I took two steps forward and one back. Other days I was only treading water, and in the early stages of my grief I did a lot of that while struggling to keep my head above the raging emotional rapids. Mourning is a journey to reclaim your balance and strength of character.

I knew I had a lot of work to do to heal my heart as you will need to do as well. The time will pass either way; it is wise to commit to the journey and decide consciously to engage in your mourning process. After going to Africa, I thought of this sojourn as a safari. The word safari is derived from a Swahili word for a "long journey usually into a remote expanse of wilderness away from your comfort zone." That seemed to describe my grief experience perfectly.

Even though it is a long trip, slowly a new and deeper harmony emerges. Confucius postulated, "It doesn't matter how slowly you go as long as you do not stop." Your inability to move is the definition of sorrow, according to Shirley MacLaine in *The Camino*, where she describes her pilgrimage. It is important to allow the time it takes to grieve. Your pilgrimage is not about reaching a specific destination. You don't really know where this trip will take you except that the side effects will be resiliency, balance, peace, joy, and health. These benefits come through perseverance within the process. I knew this would be a tough expedition, but I was determined to do it with as much grace, creativity, and style as possible. To express that determination I bought a plaque citing a quote from Ralph Waldo Emerson which read:

> *"Do not follow where the path may lead*
> *Go instead, where there is no path, and leave a trail."*

Learning to adapt is a critical tool in our world of constant change. I am reminded of the tenacious desert elephant of Namibia that learned to cope and adapt to a harsh environment by integrating into it. Claim the determination and strength of the desert elephant.

There are attributes that can help you on your expedition; it would be beneficial to pack those qualities and hone them. As you navigate this arduous journey, remember that patience, beliefs, and attitudes that support hope and wholeness will serve you well. Willingness, perseverance, a sense of humor, courage, faith, mindfulness, and resiliency will help you learn to integrate your loss into your life in the healthiest way possible. They will empower you at a time when you feel powerless.

Patience

Patience is a potent form of love, not only for others but for self as well. Endeavor to have patience with yourself. Don't expect that you can immediately function on the level you did prior to your loved one's death. I know you still must carry on with the responsibilities of life. In fact, you might have found them all put on your lone plate as I did. I discovered that things which would have been a snap to handle before Frank died became monumental tasks afterwards. I decided to look more closely at the word *responsibility*: response ability. Your ability to respond varies with your state of mind and the circumstances in which you find yourself. Cut yourself some slack. Be gentle, tender, and tolerant with yourself, and praise yourself for any step you accomplish right now as you recalibrate. Sometime during your mourning process self-forgiveness and compassion might be called for. Give yourself what your loved one would have given you.

Also, be patient with the process of mourning. By now you realize this can't be shoved aside without dire consequences to your future. You also know there isn't a quick fix. I was in active grief work for a good two years, not two weeks. Some work through the process more quickly; others take longer. "Don't let the fear of the time it will take to accomplish something stand in the way of your doing it. The time will pass anyway; we might just as well put the passing time to the best possible use," declared Earl Nightingale. Don't be passive.

Be patient with non-grievers who haven't experienced a loss as grand as yours; they usually just don't understand what you are going through. As for fellow grievers, allow them to grieve in their own way and on their unique path.

Beliefs

Your beliefs and attitudes are crucial, not only for your grief process, but for your life as well! Look at the beliefs you hold concerning death and grieving. Look at what you have been told or what has been modeled for you. If you hold the belief, *I can never get through this terrible loss or get beyond this pain*, you won't. Your thoughts are self-fulfilling prophecies. Such limiting thoughts are like negative prayers. Expect that you WILL get through the agony, not around it but through it. If you believe mourning lasts only a couple of weeks or a month, you are setting yourself up for disappointment. You might bury your turbulent feelings and thoughts and try to move on as though you are fine, but more than likely you know at your core that you're not fine and think you never will be again. It is very doubtful that stuffing your feelings down will ever lead to your being whole again. Ideally, your beliefs and attitudes should support you through this time of transition, not create barriers to growth and wholeness.

Attitude is more important than the facts of a situation. Choose your attitudes and beliefs wisely. You can *choose* them, you know. You can rewrite the scripts that you allow to run your life. Deepak Chopra says, "Every time you are tempted to react in the same old way, ask if you want to be a prisoner of the past or a pioneer of the future." Many of my well-intentioned family members and friends encouraged me to return to management consulting work after Frank died in order to make "real money" with a salary. I had left that career many years before and was currently doing massage and energy work without a set income. I chose to believe that I could provide for myself by following my heart and doing what I loved to do even with the circumstances in my life. My belief was a self-fulfilling prophecy. Be strong-hearted. You can only change your thoughts and beliefs in the present. This is the place of power. Anchor and ground into the present, the NOW. You can change your mind if what you believe isn't supporting and uplifting you. How are your beliefs affecting you in this tumultuous time of transition? For instance, if you lost your partner and are feeling inadequate on your own, you probably hold the belief that you can only be whole in a relationship. Are there wiser guidelines you could choose to live by that would empower you? You *can* redesign your blueprint!

In the course *Living Through Loss,* Marilyn Grosboll encouraged us to hold the belief that within each loss there is some gold. At first that was difficult for me to swallow. How could there be anything approximating gold in losing a loved one? She encouraged each of us to attempt acceptance of our situation rather than expend so much energy resisting that which we could not change, and then see if we could identify the "gold." I suggest you open the door to the possibility at this stage and begin to keep your senses open to signs of gold showing up in the mud. Look to your past. Did something good come of any losses or difficulties in your life? Did you grow as a person?

My father lost his job because he advocated non-military uses of the laser after he developed a laser lab at a prominent company in the 70s. The gold in this situation was the result that, with encouragement, my dad got his law degree at age forty-five, a dream he'd had for a long time. As I mentioned before, I learned at age thirty that I couldn't have children. Frank and I could have pounded on that closed door and stayed miserable, but we chose to see what other doorways opened for us. We quit our careers at the age of thirty-seven, backpacked around the world for a year, and then settled on the Greek island of Paros. That would have been possible with children, but much more difficult.

In Marilyn's course we were given a magnet with a picture of a bird in a cage struggling mightily to pry apart the bars in order to escape, when all the while there were no bars at all behind him. This was to remind us to look for what opportunity might present itself as some options become unavailable. To remind us to keep looking for the gold in a situation, Marilyn distributed a picture depicting what first looked like the profile of a duck's head, but as we continued to stare at it a rabbit appeared, looking in the opposite direction. Marilyn admonished us not to deny the duck (the situation), but to keep looking for our rabbit (the gold). As an example, Mary, a disabled woman in our class who was confined to a wheelchair, made a rabbit out of the duck of her situation by creating a job that required her to travel around the world writing articles about the difficulties of traveling with a disability. There is always some gold or something positive if we look. What can you learn from this and how can you grow from it?

I consciously chose to believe that I was experiencing a devastating loss, but being a victim was not going to be my new identity. I decided to become a heroine instead. I was determined to **become an unbreakable survivor**. People can be in the same circumstances and have different outcomes according to whether they respond consciously and mindfully or merely react. Allowing your loss to destroy the rest of your life is not a healthy option and not what your loved one would want. Marilyn said in one of our *Living Through Loss* classes, "Don't limit your challenge, rather challenge your limits." I began to think of the challenges I faced as opportunities to grow.

Dr. Viktor Frankl, an Austrian psychiatrist who was held by the Nazis at Auschwitz and subjected to many atrocities, discovered that even though the Nazis had murdered his wife and his parents, the SS guards could not control his attitude. In his inspiring book *Man's Search for Meaning* he shares how we can transform personal tragedy into triumph. He illustrates with his own life that even after horrific life situations, with hope one can find meaning in life. He is a prime example of one staying connected to their invincible resilient heart within.

One day as I was walking to a grief support gathering I noticed a lovely vine of purple morning glories. Nearby I saw a sign in a coffee shop: "I am one who eats his breakfast gazing at morning glories." I immediately thought morning glories and began playing with the concept of "mourning" glory. Glory is defined as "praise, honor, great beauty, triumph." I chose then to believe that I could experience "mourning" glory and that I would ultimately triumph. I wasn't going to experience this much pain for nothing! I began to see affirmations of this ability to choose everywhere I looked. One of the cards in *Angel Blessings* by Kimberly Marooney says, "God has given us free choice to express either limitations or divinity."

I leave this statement from Viktor Frankl for you to ponder: "The last of human freedoms – the ability to choose one's attitude in a given set of circumstances." Will you let this death finish you or will you choose to constructively work through it? You have a choice.

Willingness

Willingness is crucial on your journey. You are at a crossroads in your life. You can sit down and resist the reality that has been sprung upon you. But perhaps a better choice is to be open and take steps that will lead you through your anguish. Take a risk by stepping into the unknown. You may choose to sit with your sorrow for a while, but I encourage you to begin your *Resilient Heart*® Journey soon. A woman shared about the death of her son with such rawness and cutting pain that I assumed his death had happened very recently. As she continued to speak at the support group we learned he died *ten* years earlier. She wanted us to know that she had blocked her grief and it had negatively affected all areas of her life including her marriage. She was now ready to face her grief and she strongly implored us to do the same. Grief doesn't have a shelf life and will sit and wait for you to face it. It isn't going away and it will take its toll if not embraced and processed.

Be willing to face your fears and terrifying thoughts without resistance. I know this will take courage and fortitude; I am here to show you that this is possible. Rather than resisting the rather depressing music that you are hearing in your head at this point in time, life can eventually become a harmonious dance flowing with new, more uplifting musical phrases and notes.

In *Gift from the Sea,* Anne Morrow Lindbergh wrote these profound words about suffering: "I do not believe that sheer suffering teaches. If suffering alone taught, the entire world would be wise since everyone suffers. To suffering must be added mourning, understanding, patience, love, openness and the willingness to remain vulnerable."

I had never felt so vulnerable in my life. At times such as this I frequently selected a card at random from Kimberly Marooney's deck of *Angel Blessings,* and had total faith that the message was one I needed to hear. This time it was Zacharael who presented himself, representing surrender. It read:

"The thought of surrender is frightening at first. If we have no experience with this, we can only relate to a feeling of helplessness and vulnerability... Your faith in the angels, a power greater than yourself, the ultimate truth, Jesus, or whatever is meaningful for you provides the bridge...Surrendering is about choosing to tear your walls of separation down forever, to enter into eternal unity with God...You feel a tremendous amount of relief as you give up the fight to stay separate and relax into your Eternal Self... You give up wanting your life a certain way and allow God to direct you... True surrender is good and feels like the world has been lifted off your shoulders."

During my first year of mourning, a friend told me that my allowing lent grace to my grief experience. Most people think of grace as a gift received without effort. I think it can also supplement your effort or fill in when you can't. During this period of time I was blessed to find the book *The Power of Now* by Eckhart Tolle. His book helped me so much and came to me right when I needed it the most. Regarding acceptance he writes:

"To offer no resistance to life is to be in a state of grace, ease, and lightness." He advises yielding to the flow of life rather than opposing it.

Five months after Frank's death I wrote the following poem. Just writing it helped me to clarify my situation and my determination to accept and surrender to what was and what I could not change.

Phoenix Rising

Death is a midwife for my new life.
I've been stretched to extreme by her.
My heart exploded, shattered,
leaving a deep gaping wound
in the center of my being.
Suffering is the catalyst
to the challenge;
the challenge to birth my expanded self
through the openness,
this sacred space.
Meanwhile, I'll dance in the
darkness of my sadness,
swim in the ocean of my tears,
give voice to my screaming feelings,
and purify through fire.
For the birth of new existence,
I surrender and await the Phoenix's rising.

You must be willing to stick with your mourning work…
and it will take perseverance. Franklin D. Roosevelt said, "When
you get to the end of your rope, tie a knot and hang on." I use a
dragonfly to symbolize and remind me to hang on. In my thirties
I went through several challenges all at once: a friend was dying
of cancer; another friend was going through a rough divorce, and
my father-in-law had a stroke while visiting us in New Jersey. I
came very close to burnout because I didn't take care of myself
as I supported others. When I realized that I was quickly reaching
my wit's end, I finally retreated to my parents' lake home to
regain my own health and well-being. I loved to walk in solitude
in the fields there. On the first day I noticed a dragonfly clinging

to a stick in the tall grass. Day after day that dragonfly clung tenaciously to that stick, even in fierce winds. I decided if he could withstand the buffeting, I could too. I told my family about the dragonfly and though I didn't express it, I feared that when my father went out to mow the field while I was away he would cut down the dragonfly's perch as well. To my surprise and joy he found the stick and left a large swath of uncut grass around it. My dad didn't say "I love you" very often, but that simple act shouted it to me! Since then the dragonfly has become a symbol in our family for holding on and persevering. The family coat of arms contains the motto "Hold Fast" and now I associate those words with the dragonfly.

Mindfulness

A few years after Frank died I found this powerful poem written by Rashani Réa, founder of Kipukamaluhia Sanctuary on the Big Island of Hawaii:

The Unbroken

There is a brokenness
out of which comes the unbroken,
a shatteredness
out of which blooms the unshatterable.
There is a sorrow
beyond all grief which leads to joy
and a fragility
out of whose depths emerges strength.

There is a hollow space
too vast for words
through which we pass with each loss,
out of whose darkness
we are sanctioned into being.

There is a cry deeper than all sound
whose serrated edges cut the heart
as we break open to the place inside
which is unbreakable and whole,
while learning to sing.

Mindfulness is imperative to move us from broken to that which is unbreakable. Awareness is an essential part of transformation. It is the lack of mindfulness that is causing you, as it did me, to not be present, and that creates havoc in our lives. Being mindful puts us back in the driver's seat, looking forward rather than backward when we navigate through life. It is very important that we face our loss with mindful attention. I suggest you practice becoming a greater witness to your thoughts, your feelings, and your actions. The inner witness observes with keen insight. I consider this witness to be a spark of Divinity that resides in your heart. It is still there even when your heart explodes with pain from loss. It is that unbreakable and "unshatterable" gem within: It will never abandon you. This is your *Resilient Heart*®. It often speaks to you through your intuition, your inner knowing. It is important to learn to hear the voice of your heart. You might already be listening within. If not, I recommend that you cultivate an open relationship with your inner being. It is your built-in guidance system or GPS and can wisely guide you. I gave you an example earlier when I emotionally dissolved on the grocery store floor. It was the part of me that realized what was taking place and gave me permission to persevere. It is a raft to cling to as you are swept down a raging river. It allows you to step out of the mayhem and realistically gauge what is going on. You may choose to jump back in the rapids, but you are then doing it consciously. There is a big difference between doing something by choice rather than just reacting. Work to stay present and attentive.

During my period of grief, I scheduled times to check in with myself. Each week I took stock of my thoughts, feelings, actions, and what was going on in my body. I reviewed my mourning journey at six months and then annually for several years after. Here is a portion of what I wrote in my journal six months into my grief period:

> *At six months I am beginning to feel more stable and less fractured. But I find within this stability incredible waves of even deeper pain course through me. They grip me. I recall when Frank first died; it was all too big, too painful to assimilate. I couldn't absorb the magnitude of my loss. Now that full spectrum of knowingness of the deep loss is showing up to be accepted, embraced, and integrated into my being.*

I also journaled that I decided I needed a brain transplant since mine didn't seem to be functioning. I constantly did things without being mindful like locking myself out of my apartment and having to break back in through a very high bathroom window. Another example of not being present I shared with you earlier was that I repeatedly locked my car with the engine running and the key in the ignition. Where was my brain? What had happened to my rational thinking process?

Strive to give yourself the priceless gift of presence. Think about how different it feels when you are with someone and they are totally attentive to you and completely present, compared to being with an individual who is there physically, but the rest of them is somewhere else. They are mentally abandoning you. **Don't abandon yourself.** Endeavor to weave a strong presence of attentiveness to yourself into the fabric of your life. If you have children grieving alongside you they will also need your presence. By modeling how you are attentive to your thoughts, feelings, and actions, you are teaching them a valuable lesson about the grieving process for them to adopt into their lives as well.

Sense of Humor

When I was a child my mother taught me to pack a sense of humor for my life journey. She shared how laughter helped her to cope with challenges throughout her life. She was a very wise woman. This is a time of deep sorrow, but don't forget to bring your sense of humor on this pilgrimage; you'll need it to integrate your profound loss. My dear Frank was able to retain his sense of humor almost until his last breath. I took him for colonics because no medications were helping with his chronic constipation. On the first visit he told Debra, the compassionate colonic therapist, that she had a really tough job ahead of her. Seeing her confused expression, he declared, "Well, I've been a lawyer for about twenty-five years and you know how full of it they are!" We all laughed and it cut the tension.

I decided if Frank could keep his ability to see the lightness in a situation while dying, I would try to do the same after he died.

Laughter is an energetic discharge, like crying. It seemed a very long time before I laughed as I previously had. I wrote this in my journal:

> *Today I was thinking how I have received compliments on my laugh and laughter all my life. I miss laughing with Frank. Our days were filled with laughter. We would wake up and be happy. Now I don't laugh on my own, except at myself. We were often told how people laughed so much more when we were around. I hear other couples laughing together and my heart yearns for the sound of our laughter.*

Recently I was speaking with a friend who shared that after a long dark period of her soul, she heard a strange sound. It took several seconds to realize that the sound was coming from herself: it was her own laughter! It had been so long since she had allowed herself that joy that when she heard that beautiful sound she knew she was finally healing. I learned to laugh more, and not just at myself, but that still happens frequently! Once again I am often told by friends that they laugh more when I'm around. A few years after Frank passed, dear friends of ours told me that they thought my tears and laughter during Frank's illness and death and my ability to see the funny side of life and death was a great lesson to them. I had vowed to keep my sense of humor and their observation let me know I had lived up to it.

Some people feel it is disrespectful to laugh or to feel the least bit of joy after someone they love dies. I disagree. **Blocking any emotion stifles them all.** Allow what wants to flow to flow. It is healthy to laugh and that's a scientific fact. Harriet Hodgson wrote an article and referred to a study by the Mayo Clinic about the importance of laughter, on the site www. Centering.org. "Laughter makes you take in more 'oxygen-rich air' and stimulates the heart, lungs and muscles. It increases the endorphins in the brain, which affect your mood and improves your immune system." Laughter is medicinal for the soul as well. I recommend regular doses.

Dark comedy, or black humor, makes light of what is often a solemn subject matter; wit and discomfort are simultaneously experienced. Bruce, a friend, lost his dog Ira, and was distraught. His friend tried to contain her laughter, but blurted out, "It's the end of an Ira." They both burst into laughter. Bruce told me it was as good as crying to get the emotion to flow. About nine months after Frank died my friend Roseanne and I watched the movie *The Sixth Sense* on TV. When I realized at the end of the movie that the husband was actually dead and that it was his ghost that had been trying to communicate with his wife I began sobbing hysterically. Roseanne held me through this catharsis. Eventually, my inner witness tuned into the present and I realized that the movie credits had played and now a John Phillip Sousa march was being broadcast in a commercial. When I finally swam up from my tears and grasped the absurdity of crying to a Sousa march I switched instantly from blubbering to explosive laughter. The emotional release from the tears and then the laughter was so cleansing it was like taking a deep lungful of cool morning air and exhaling with force! Erma Bombeck, that witty newspaper columnist and author who used humor to describe the American suburban home life, wrote, "If you can't make it better, you can laugh at it."

Bringing your sense of humor on your mourning journey can help you cope and release difficult emotions.

Courage

You will need courage to face the rigors of grief. I asked for renewed courage in order to consciously experience, without the benefit of anesthesia (drugs, alcohol, etc.) the difficult and intense emotions I was having. Often I would be disheartened and discouraged by the daunting task ahead. The word *courage* is derived from the Anglo-French *coeur* or heart. Seeing the origin of the word courage helped me to understand how difficult it was to be courageous with such a wounded heart. Theodore Roosevelt is quoted as having said, "Courage is not having the strength to go on; it is going on when you don't have the strength!" And Mary Anne Radmacher echoed, "Courage doesn't always roar. Sometimes courage is the little voice at the end of the day that says I'll try again tomorrow." Having courage doesn't mean you have no fear. In fact for you to be courageous there must be fear. I felt a lot of fear in grief and I often needed support to rekindle my courage either from friends, family, or my faith. I regularly recited the Serenity Prayer written by American theologian Reinhold Niebuhr, a prayer that I have loved since childhood: "God grant me the serenity to accept the things I cannot change, the courage to change the things I can, and the wisdom to know the difference."

It takes tremendous valor to move on after such a loss, to take even one step into the unknown. During such trauma, the first quality to be tested is your faith. Hold fast to your faith because it may need strengthening during the leveling process of grief. Trust your heart, for it knows. Listen within, breathe, and take a step. Have faith in yourself and the process. You'll need to take it one day at a time as you rebuild connection to your *Resilient Heart*®. With time you'll discover that you do have the strength to face your future and you'll slowly rediscover more harmony in your life. Have courage and you will learn to see in the darkness. Leon Bloy, the French novelist and poet said, "There are places in the heart which do not yet exist, and into them enters suffering that they may have existence." **Try desperately not to close your heart. Let your heart heal in the exploded state, allowing for expansion.**

Early in my grief I opened a fortune cookie and the message was a quote from Elmer Fudd: "Be bwave wittle wabbit, be bwave!" I kept it in my wallet for years as a reminder to be brave. I also bought a cute *wittle* stuffed *wabbit* with patches on his body as my mascot. He is here on my desk as I write this book.

You now know what to expect on your *Resilient Heart*® Journey and what assets or internal resources you should take along with you. You know it is not a short and easy trip or one you can bypass or sit out. This would be a good time to review how you have coped with other losses or challenges in your life. It doesn't matter that they were not as monumental as this loss; you can gain insight into what worked for you in the past. You can detect signs of patience, empowering beliefs, willingness, mindfulness, humor, and courage that you have already displayed. You carry the seeds of resiliency within, although perhaps they aren't currently sprouting. You have the ability to recover and be strong. You are invincible by nature. Hold on!

As encouragement, remember these words from Traci L. Slatton's book *Immortal:* "Boy, the solid things you can hold in your hands are never all you've got. They're the least of what belong to you. The qualities inside you, those are what you've really got to defend yourself with."

Heartfelt Suggestions

Now it is time to go to a quiet place where you can take some time for yourself. Bring a notebook and pen. Place your hand over your heart and close your eyes. Take several slow deep breaths down into your lower belly. Allow your breath to guide you to the peaceful place within your heart. Now open your eyes and begin reading and reflect on the suggestions. This is part of your conscious mourning and it is sacred work.

1. Are you telling your story either verbally or through writing, e.g. in a blog or journal?

2. Are any past losses resurfacing?

3. Are you experiencing more than one loss right now?

4. Can you relate to the idea of "dancing in the dark?"

5. Are you feeling resistance to accept the death you are grieving? If so, how is it revealing itself?

6. Do you feel like you don't recognize yourself since the death? How are you different?

7. How patient are you being with yourself?

8. What are your beliefs concerning death and grieving? What has been taught to you or modeled about such a loss?

9. Will your beliefs about death and grief empower you for mourning?

10. Are your attitudes supporting you in a positive way right now?

11. Look at past losses you have experienced. Can you see any gold? Can you find any rabbits in the duck of those situations?

12. What did you learn?

13. How did you grow?

14. Commit to checking on your progress as you grieve: weekly, at six months, and annually. Look at how you are feeling, your self-talk, how you are taking care of yourself, and examine your behavior.

15. Have you seen any sign of your sense of humor? If not, I strongly suggest you go search for it and reclaim it.

CHAPTER THREE

RELATING: Cocooning and Connecting

GRIEVING AFFECTS HOW YOU CONNECT with yourself and others. Loss leaves you a changed person, trying to find your way in your shattered reality. It can be quite difficult to relate even to yourself, let alone other people. Many don't feel comfortable around any aspect of death and are unsure of how to communicate with you. On the other hand, individuals whom you might not have known before, but who have gone through such a tragedy themselves, can and do relate to you. You somehow find each other, often in the most unlikely places, like the vegetable department of a grocery store or in a copy shop. After Frank died I made a memorial candle in his honor and was at a copy shop getting duplicates made of my favorite photos of him to glue on the outer glass. When another customer asked me what I was doing and I explained, she told me that her mom had recently died and that she was creating a memorial photo collage. We stood there and cried together. It was a heartfelt connection.

Another day I went to the bank to open an account in my name only. That seemingly simple act drove home the finality of Frank's death and brought me to tears once more as I sat talking with the banker. He was so understanding, compassionate, and supportive when I shared why I was crying. These soulful encounters were sincere and authentic heart-to-heart experiences which illustrated to me how united we actually are. I made these amazing connections during Frank's illness and after his death. I had always felt intellectually that we are all one, but through these seemingly "coincidental" meetings I learned that it really is true. No matter where we live on this planet we all share the same basic needs for love, relationship, shelter, and food. We all suffer if a loved one dies. The only guarantee that comes with birth is death, so most of us will suffer such a profound loss at least once in our lifetime.

I knew instinctively during my mourning that I needed that connection and support more than ever. I celebrated when I felt it and also knew when I needed to create it. I have a small yet incredibly supportive family and circle of caring friends. I leaned on them. I realized that I needed assistance to walk this difficult journey so I also sought the right grief support group for me.

Ask for grace and assistance. Frank and I had always found it easier to give than receive. With his illness, we both found ourselves in a vulnerable place where we had to learn to receive, to be willing to accept support from others. As a culture we pride ourselves in being strong and self-sufficient. If we are authentic, then there will be times when we do need help which is okay. I have never felt more delicate in my life as I did after Frank died. I needed help to remind me how to rebuild myself and I needed cheerleaders to encourage me throughout this process.

Through the love and support I was receiving, which in turn lead to the comprehension that we truly are one family in Spirit. I was moved to express it through poetry:

Connections
Our lives are interconnected,
each a facet of the whole.
Mainstay through challenge.
Grace and blessings of chance meetings
and true friends of duration,
all wonderful people who touch my life
and buoy my soul!

I also painted a mandala to depict my supportive network of people. A mandala is a circular painting. The outer edge of my circle is comprised of a ring of purple hearts, representing bravery, and between each one you see the top of a person's head facing the center of the circle and their outstretched arms connect them. The hands of each of the six people hold a corner of a hexagon, which symbolizes integration, harmony, and balance in sacred geometry. Sacred geometry is based on the idea that geometric shapes have spiritual and symbolic meaning. Within the hexagon I drew a six-pointed star, also a sacred geometrical symbol, to create a net. In the center of the net is a naked woman to represent me in a vulnerable state being supported and held. My mandala incorporated all of the elements and symbolism that I was feeling.

Family

If it is a family member who has just passed, then you are not the only one grieving. Keep in mind that each of you may be grieving in a completely different manner, and it is easy to judge someone who mourns in another way. Remember that you wouldn't want to be criticized for the way in which you show your own grief. I've seen couples break up due to mourning differences. One presumes that the other just couldn't have loved the one they've lost as much as they did because they aren't showing their despair in the same way. Not only do people have a different style of dealing with sorrow, but they can hold different beliefs about the process. One can think that life should return to normal quite quickly after experiencing a death in the family while another realizes that is impossible for them.

Tolerance and communication are crucial during this stressful time. Strive to listen to each other from your heart, not just with your ears. You can grow in understanding each other and if you think you need help, seek out the right counselor to assist you through these challenging times. It might be through a church, another spiritual source, or through hospice. You might find that a private counselor works best for you. You don't hesitate taking your car to a specialist if it needs a tune up, do you? Most of us at some time in our lives need help – an emotional tune up, if you will, or a complete overhaul as I needed!

I had no family living near me in California while I mourned, but my only sibling, my sister Velvet, called me daily from Texas where she lives. Velvet is six years younger than I, but during this traumatic time, she announced she would be the older sister for me for a while. Later we decided we would step into that role as needed for each other. She is a counselor by profession, so her support and guidance were priceless and our bond grew so strong during this time. I am very fortunate to have Velvet in my life.

My father and I sometimes had a difficult time relating before Frank's death. Each time I would visit I would be determined not to let him push my buttons... and then they were pushed yet again. But after Frank died I changed the "game." I quit playing by not reacting at all. His critical words landed on deaf ears. It all seemed so stupid to me. Here is an excerpt from my journal:

> *Then there is the tax return that is due, hanging over my head on my 'to do' list. This will be my first one, since Frank handled that responsibility. Dad said he would help me, but then he starts speaking with anger and talking to me like I'm a moron. He is really helping me... yeah! Finally last night on the phone I stayed centered and explained he had to quit talking to me like that. I went on to explain that I am in a fragile state and this wasn't helping. He laughed. I retorted that it wasn't funny and I was very serious. I felt a shift happen within me, a change for the better.*

I found that I spoke up more for my needs after my loss. I also didn't settle for superficial conversations. I wanted depth and authenticity in my relationships and definitely no silly games. Such trauma clearly defines your values.

You might have young or grown children who are grieving alongside you. My nine-year-old niece Brittney and her older brother, Chad, who was seventeen at the time, were very close to Frank and adored him. Brittney made cards and wrote many letters to Frank when he was ill, filled with images of hammers hitting and destroying cancer cells. She told him that she would love him forever and that she would take care of the family. When Frank died, Brittney was devastated. She attended the celebration of his life and we encouraged her to help arrange things and be involved. For some time afterward Brittney would play a particular song that reminded her of her Uncle Frank and she would dance and cry.

One of my roles with hospice volunteer work was to co-facilitate a group called *I Count, Too*, for children who were grieving the loss of a parent, sibling, grandparent, or someone close to them. Our group was open to all grieving children in the community, not only for those whose loved one had died in hospice. Too often children are not included in the grief process and they feel isolated. Some children find it very difficult to grieve until they see the adults around them return to some semblance of balance; they may feel a sense of protection toward the griever. A dear friend of mine lost her twin brother when they were about six years old and the family never explained to her that he died. He was just gone and wasn't coming back. Some families think they are protecting the child by not sharing relevant facts about death, but that doesn't honor their feelings and only adds to their confusion. I recall one girl who lost her mother and she drew a picture of herself way off to the side of all the activities of the death that she depicted.

We gave the children many different ways to express their feelings: writing letters to the departed loved one, painting, working with clay to express their angst, writing notes to the deceased then putting them in a balloon and releasing them. There were opportunities for them to verbalize their pain and concerns. Remember, as you grieve, you are teaching your children how to handle loss in their lives by what you say and model. I believe it is good for them to see that you are dealing with pain rather than putting on a mask. Children need to see that you are trying to function, even if not as fully as before. They often understand more than you realize. If you are too swamped with your own grief to help your children though theirs, find some support for them as they deal with their own experience of great loss. It is a good idea to let their school counselor know about the death with which they are struggling to come to terms.

It helped a lot that my nephew was older than his sister. Besides assisting me in organizing the estate sale, he helped sort through Frank's clothes. This was too difficult for me to handle. If you have older children they can help you through this ordeal. As you let them support you it also helps them with their grief.

I want to discuss the possibility that you might have experienced some horrific happenings around the death or funeral of your loved one. A death in the family brings out the best and the worst in people: greed can show its ugly face. I saw some prime examples of this behavior during and after my father-in-law's funeral. I was shocked at some of the conduct and the things said. Before my mother died, she told my sister and me that if we ever argued about any THING after she died she would come back to haunt us. We didn't; our relationship is more important than any THING.

Greed isn't the only issue that can cause family friction. Disagreeing about treatments or the decision to leave or take someone off of life support can create a fracture in a family. The bottom line is you must decide how much of the discord was due to heightened emotions because of the circumstances and how important this relationship is to you. Avoid destructive relationships at a time when you are desperately trying to fill your emotional needs. In fact, it's healthy to avoid those kinds of relationships at any time in your life.

Friends

Some African tribes have a beautiful tradition of singing a song when a child is born. This song becomes the child's song and follows them throughout their life. The community sings this song to remind them who they are should they go down a bad path or experience trauma or loss. The song is also sung again at their death.

During grief I often forgot who I truly was and needed to be reminded of my song. Often it was my family and my friends who did that. They sang my essence back to me so I could remember who I was and slowly put the pieces together again. Friends have always been important to me, but they became life-preservers and champions while I was trying to structure my new life. I received cards, letters, and phone calls from many people. Of course, that lessened with time, but never completely ceased. I have some very loyal friends and compassionate people who care about me. I feel very blessed to make that declaration.

I was the first in my circle of friends to lose a partner and yet some seemed to truly understand the gut-wrenching pain with which I struggled. When my self-esteem plummeted, they expressed how they saw me, which was so different than my perspective of me at the time. When I could only see what I was currently laboring with, they saw my overall strength. They saw grace when I felt so ungraceful, more like a floundering fish out of water. Grief mires everything. I was told that I was courageous and brave when I so needed to hear those words. A dear friend gave me three candles and a note which read, "Gently hang on as you let go!" Sometimes they got me to laugh, usually as I shared my latest antic. People said that I was teaching them how to deal with death and they were proud of me. One friend emailed me, writing, "I am so glad you are creating opportunities for healing. I love you for taking the time and using the energy to heal." One year after Frank's death, the end of the most difficult year of my life, I was sitting at a table with friends when one announced, "Gail, you already have what all of us at this table are looking for: inner harmony." I needed this feedback and support as much as a drowning person needs a rescuing hand.

Unfortunately, during this period of my life two close friendships dissolved. They both repeatedly disappointed me when I needed to count on their word. They hurt me deeply at a time when I was most vulnerable.

I noted in my journal that it took me six months before I could reach out and call someone. I just couldn't do it. I had such a need to cocoon and regroup, and I wasn't feeling very social. I needed some solitude to lick my gaping wounds and mend my bleeding heart. Thank goodness my friends called me and stayed in contact during that phase. My friends held that needed space and enveloped me in love while I healed.

I did go with a friend to an art show and performance and I saw many people I hadn't seen since before Frank died. Some didn't even know of his death. At least three individuals apologized for their tears. As my tears flowed as well, I let them know that they were sharing in my grief and their tears were honoring the man they cared about. True friends cry with you as well as laugh with you.

I realized that by example I was helping others on their path during my grief. Among those beautiful quotes by unknown authors is this one: "Friends are angels who lift us to our feet when our wings have trouble remembering how to fly." We were remembering how to fly together. I did a Reiki session for a woman in my *Growing Through Loss* course and she said it made the difference in how she centered herself and spoke from her heart at a life-changing meeting as she bought a new business. A year after Frank died of lung cancer I went to visit my good friend George in Florida who was also dying with the same disease. As such strong emotions rose up within me I realized how our friends felt when they came to see Frank during his illness. It was such a wonderful way to give back, visiting with my old friend. Even while you are on your mourning trek, look for ways you can reach out to others. A side effect of helping others is that it assists your own healing.

Support Groups

Support groups are worth checking out. Maybe this is for you, maybe not. I know that once I found the right ones for me, they assisted me in processing my loss and integrating it into my life. They helped me to begin to redesign my life without my loved one. It helped me to hear others' stories and how they were coping with their loss. It was also a perfect place for me to share my story and my attempts at expressing my intense and scary emotions. The two way communication was like mouth to mouth resuscitation. I could see firsthand that I wasn't going crazy, or at least I wasn't the only one going wacko. I saw that so many of my bizarre thoughts, feelings, and behaviors were normal after a loss through death. I knew that every Thursday at 5:30 pm I could share and/or cry in a safe and nurturing environment. I found that if I expressed my emotions openly and freely there, then I didn't erupt in inappropriate places or at less than ideal times. It was a perfect place to let out the steam of my grief before my pot overflowed. It was also the place I could share my beautiful memories of Frank.

The main group I attended was Marilyn Grosboll's *Growing Through Loss* course that I referred to earlier in this book. The group was for individuals who had experienced a variety of losses, not just death. There were also individuals going through divorce, experiencing loss of their health, loss of their job, or any loss that caused grief. We were all on the same journey, but for different reasons. Marilyn also taught us coping skills. She created a safe and private space for us. It was a confidential place as well. No one was required to share and some never did. I forced myself to share each week and felt such relief doing so. I took the course for five semesters. I kept telling Marilyn that I hadn't passed yet as I showed up yet again. **It is important to**

have someone witness your pain; a grief course or support group can give you that opportunity.

I originally attended these sessions for solace and guidance for myself, but discovered that I was also giving to others through soulful sharing and being creative with my mourning. One woman told me that she had been very passive in her mourning but became determined to become more fully engaged in her process after hearing me speak. To be of service to others has always been a priority of mine, but I was taken aback that I was able to do that during this time of my life. It is amazing how when you are at your lowest and while thinking how desperately *you* need help, you can still uplift others.

I believe when you are authentic and share from your depth, you automatically touch others. By being completely open and honest, doors open to intimacy and deep connection. Yes, it is very formidable to be so transparent, vulnerable, and broken open, but that is honestly where you might find yourself. Sharing the truth of where you are can benefit yourself and others. In these support sessions by inspiring and motivating one another, we took turns rekindling each other's flames of healing, so needed in the darkness of grief. In a Greek myth, Ariadne gives her lover Theseus a spool of thread to follow and it leads him out of the labyrinth to avoid the Minataur, thus saving him. You don't know what piece of the puzzle you might be providing to help guide others through the arduous labyrinth of loss. I realized that I was already beginning to fulfill Frank's desire: that his illness and death help others in some way.

I attended a widow and widower support group through hospice. That helped me, but I was uncomfortable with one thing: some of the participants seemed to be stuck in their grief. Some were still attending five years after their loss! Some only did things with other grievers; they seemed to segregate themselves. It appeared that grief had become their new identity and lifestyle. I observed that some clung to the role of victim. It evidently worked for them, but that wasn't the path I wanted to take. I believe we all feel like victims at first. We ask *Why us? Why now? Why me?* However, there comes a time when you must forge a new identity and live your remaining years fully. Yes, we must allow our grief to flow and feel it in order to be able to move on, but there is a big difference between feeling it and clinging to it indefinitely. Right from the beginning, I held fast to the determination to be a survivor. I made that commitment long before I began the conscious journey, but the goal was set. I wondered, at times with great doubt and tremendous fear, how I could get through it. Yet I was determined to live through this and even grow through it. You must decide what your path will be. I have seen individuals who used self-pity as an excuse to do nothing. Transformation is possible when grief is embraced with resilience. There is no right or wrong way to mourn; however, I do advise you to do it constructively and consciously.

I am in the process of creating an online support group. I invite you to visit www.GailSaunders.com to learn more about this group. There are so many options, and it is easier to find what is best for you with the available technologies of today. There are other online support groups as well so if this idea resonates with you, by all means do check it out.

I also found I needed support for areas of my life that I couldn't handle on my own while in mourning. I normally meditated, but had difficulty doing it on my own after Frank died, so I signed up for a course in breathing meditation to walk me back into something I knew would benefit me. I had taught such courses before, but now I needed encouragement; I needed guidance. I signed up for a journal-writing course and an art therapy course. I joined a barter club and offered my massage and energy work in exchange for learning many of the skills I was lacking, especially working with computers (I was totally challenged in computers and technology when I found myself single). This worked very well for me and the exchanges didn't have to be direct. I got credit for my work and could apply it to the huge list of possible services. Figure out what can help you. Find guidance, if you need it. This is part of conscious, constructive, and creative mourning.

Communicating with Non-Grievers

If you want support from certain people, tell them a bit about the process of mourning so that they know what to expect from you during your journey. Tell them that this is the roughest loss or the worst thing that has ever happened to you. Explain that it will take a while for you to integrate it into your being and life. Warn them that you might not be your normal self for quite a while. Tell them that your emotions are intensified right now so they will be aware of this fact. Let them know that you might have trouble reaching out, but you still need them to support you and love you. Share with them that their concern and care are precious gifts for you and that you will survive this with their help. Sometimes non-grievers say things that hurt. It isn't intentional – they just don't understand. Both my father and a friend kept pushing for me to return to full-time work sooner than I was prepared to do. When I told my friend I wasn't ready yet he asked if I needed medication. I responded, "That is the last thing I need. I am sleeping, I am functioning, and I need to feel my emotions to process them."

A friend shared with me that the day after her mother's funeral she sat on her bed sobbing. Her boyfriend entered the room and asked why she was so upset. She reminded him that her mom just died. He responded, "Oh. I guess you're not over it yet." It is often necessary to clarify what others can expect while you mourn your deep loss, what can be normal behavior (even if they might disagree), and that you need support.

Heartfelt Suggestions

Now it is time to go to a quiet place where you can have some time with yourself. Bring a pen and notebook. Place your hand over your heart and close your eyes. Take several slow deep breaths down into your lower belly. Allow your breath to guide you to the peaceful place within your heart. Now open your eyes and begin reading and reflect on the suggestions. Remember this is part of your conscious mourning and it is sacred work.

1. Have you felt a sense of oneness? Have you experienced support and understanding from people you just met?

2. Are you able to ask for assistance from others, e.g. friends, family, and/or professionals? What help will you ask for?

3. Have things changed in any of your relationships with friends or family members since the loss of your loved one?

4. Are you speaking up for your needs and setting protective boundaries when necessary?

5. Are there children grieving alongside you? How can you help them in their process of integrating their loss? Are there older children whom you can lean on now?

6. Do you have someone to remind you of your strengths, someone to sing your song back to you?

7. Are you open to check if a support group would be right for you?

8. Do you have someone or someplace you can openly share your feelings and grief experiences?

9. Are you determined to be resilient?

10. Are there avenues, e.g. courses that could encourage and remind you to do healthy options like exercise and meditation? Are you setting up situations that will guide and spur you on when you can't do it for yourself?

11. Have you shared with non-grievers what or what not to expect from you?

Your Departed Loved One

When a person dies, the relationship doesn't; it merely changes. The individual is no longer physically with you, but you don't need to cut all ties with your loved one and you don't need to erase all of your memories. You are still connected in heart and soul, and you can create a new kind of bond with your loved one. You can still relate to them, but in a different way. I know you want the old expression of your relationship back; I did, too. Yet you also know that isn't an option, so hold fast to the precious experiences you shared and work to let go of any painful memories.

Frank and I had been married for nearly twenty-nine years and connected deeply on a daily basis. I couldn't suddenly cut off my communication with him so I wrote him many letters. Those letters helped so much to gradually integrate the truth that Frank had died. I also talked to him in my head and sometimes out loud after he died. You might feel there is unfinished business between you and your departed one. You might hold unsaid words of love, forgiveness, or even anger inside your mind and heart. You might have been robbed of the opportunity to say good-bye to them – you might even harbor regret. You can write them a letter and share your pent-up thoughts and feelings. This is not unusual; many people have shared that they do the same.

Here is one letter I wrote to Frank:

> *Hi my Darling,*
> *My life without you is like a painting with dull and blurred shades of dark pigment. Life with you, Babe, was bright lively strokes of intense vibrant color. There was a splash of red, a wild stroke of brilliant turquoise, and areas of harmonious shades of calming blues. We could share the same space and yet be engrossed in separate projects. I miss doing everything with you, even making the bed. I miss hearing us saying over and over, "Team work is the best." I miss how we prided ourselves in making even the most mundane activities fun together, like washing clothes by hand for eight years while we lived in Greece. I loved how we played while we did the sheets, laughing, and splashing each other in the process. Now I do everything alone. There is no laughter and no playing. I miss my partner in crime. Where is the zest in my life? I know you always gave me the credit for being the little engine. You said I instigated our madness and adventures. But, Babe, you created such support, a launching*

pad of encouragement. You created the grounding from which I could fly. I now feel grounded and unable to spread my wings and soar. I feel more like a phoenix in the ashes. We always said that lovers should be gardeners for each other. We should tend the soil using fertilizer, weeding, and watering so each could flourish and grow to their full potential. You, Frank, were a gardener par excellence. I think how much I've grown with your care and love. Thank you, my dear Frank! Now the challenge is to continue flowering and not die on my own. How to become my own gardener? I know you are still sending down sunlight and rain on your flower. I hear you jumping in that I am your blooming idiot. I'm laughing. I can't tell you in words how much I miss you and how empty my life feels without you beside me. Eternal love, Gail

I wanted communication from him as well. I contacted a psychic whom we had visited thirteen years prior. She was phenomenal then, but when I found her again she explained that she was fighting cancer and might not be as clear a channel, which I found to be the case. I did feel she made contact with Frank, but on a limited basis. This was only the second time I had worked with a psychic. Frank and I had gone to her the first time rather on a lark. We were very skeptical and made separate appointments so that she wouldn't know we knew each other. I liked her right away as she explained that few people who claim they are psychic really are. She added that even a good one is not 100% accurate on their best days. Throughout the session she interspersed what she referred to as tests. These were facts that weren't even in my conscious mind. For instance, my parents had lost a child during the years between my sister's birth and mine and his name would have been Gregory. I had no knowledge of this at the time, but my parents later confirmed it was true. I understand if you also want to make contact with your loved one, but be discriminating.

Through other experiences, I did receive what I consider confirmation that Frank still exists on another dimension. I feel he did make contact with me. You might have unusual experiences as well, so I will share some of mine.

One of the first things that happened occurred about a week after Frank died. I found a tape he had made for me when he was first diagnosed with incurable cancer. He had been told that he might have only two weeks to live. On the tape he told me again how much he loved me and began to sing our song, *More,* until he broke down crying. He said he would continue later, but never got the chance to finish our song. His tape is such a precious gift.

Another experience occurred four months after his death. I was deep in the stress of not only of losing him, but I was also sorting through all of our belongings to downsize from a very large three-bedroom home to a one-bedroom apartment. There was a tulip tree in the yard of that home that had blossomed as usual in March during his four-month illness. One of Frank's first symptoms was losing his sight. As it quickly graduated to blindness there was a period during which he saw things similar to the way an insect sees: duplicate, shaking images, often overlapping each other. There was a garden light illuminating the tulip tree and its blossoms looked to him like blinking, shimmering fairy lights. In August as I struggled with the move and all it entailed, three blossoms appeared overnight on the tulip tree. I knew it was a sign from Frank that he was still with me and supporting me.

On the six-month anniversary of his death I was walking alone on the deserted beach in Santa Barbara where I had returned to live. I was thinking of Frank when suddenly a perfect long-stemmed rose washed ashore at my feet from the ocean of salt water. It was the pale yellow and coral color he often bought for me. I thought, *Is this from you, Babe?* I got truth bumps of confirmation. I imagined Frank saying, "Well, who do you think it was from? Do you need a card as well?" I added the incredible experience to my journal, writing that it was a gift from Frank from my ocean of tears. Later I picked up a book that spoke of the Cherokee legend of the Trail of Tears: the mothers were grieving and crying so much because they couldn't help their children survive the journey. The elders asked for a sign that would lift their spirits and give them strength. The next day a rose was growing where each tear had fallen.

On the first Valentine's Day without Frank, a friend gave me a massage. My intention was to invite up any denied emotions and it was quite dramatic as I coughed and even began vomiting up energy. I had some major releases as I concentrated on letting go of any resistance. Then I noticed that my breathing changed to deep sighs and I felt my whole core shift and release on a deep level. Next I felt vibrations all through my body and near the end of the session I saw, with my eyes closed, a vision of a purple heart. It came closer and closer and appeared larger and larger. I thought of the Purple Heart award for courage and valor and then I realized it was a valentine from Frank. Chills of truth and tears flowed at the same time. I still get them whenever I remember this experience.

On my first birthday after Frank died, I again traded massages with a friend. I am able to totally let go while on a massage table and relax into deep levels. At the end of that session I heard Frank say to me, "Happy birthday, Darling. I give you night skies full of bright stars, blue skies full of brightly colored balloons, and fields of roses." That was the only time I've heard him speak to me. It was so clear I assumed my friend heard him too, but she didn't.

One day I was on the phone reading to a friend the vows Frank and I wrote to each other for our twenty-first anniversary when suddenly a lovely rainbow appeared on the printed vows. When I told her what I was seeing we both got chills and the tears flowed.

Almost immediately after Frank passed, I started to experience a new sensation. It began all through my body like waves of delicate chills, similar to goose bumps. It adjusted to just happening in my left leg and moving upward into my body. It is how I know Frank is with me. It is so reassuring and comforting. It happened much more often while I was in my deep mourning, but still occurs occasionally. I usually get the gift when I am upset and could use a hug or strength. We used to say, "Well, here we are," when we found ourselves in some dilemma. I found myself in a quandary recently and the old phrase popped out of my mouth, even using *we*. I corrected myself and said I meant *I*. I quickly felt my gift of Frank's presence and I knew on some level there is still a *we*.

During my first year of grief I found a card Frank mailed to me just before his illness struck. We were apart for several months as he began a new job and I finished teaching commitments in Santa Barbara. He wrote, "Out of sight, out of mind? Not a chance. From the one who loves you More." I know he still goes on, he is still conscious of me, and still loving me. As I am writing this, how appropriate that Celine Dion just came on the radio singing *My Heart Will Go On* from the movie *Titanic*.

"Good-byes are only for those who love with their eyes, because for those who love with heart and soul, there is no separation." ~ Rumi

I was preparing for my second Christmas without Frank and found it still quite difficult. I bought a tiny live tree to put on a table, but I still couldn't use the ornaments we had collected together, each representing a different year. I was desperately missing him and was surprised at the depth of pain that welled up yet again. I broke down sobbing, which was more sporadic at this point in my bereavement. I finally decided to look for some Christmas cards I had in a box. Rifling through the container I picked up a piece of paper and read, "Hi Beautiful, I love you!"

I burst into tears. This was a note from Frank that I must have kept. I composed myself and went back to the box. I picked up another piece of paper that read, "In fact, I love you more!" We had a standing argument about who loved whom the most. The tears just flowed and flowed. I know Frank guided me to those notes. When two hearts beat in harmony there is no distance between them.

Sometimes I would go to a card shop and pick out a card that I thought Frank would have bought for me. I would stand in the aisle and look for the perfect one, what I needed to hear from him. Only a couple of times did I actually buy one. During other times when I wished he were there to advise me about something, I would get quiet and think what he would say to me if he could. I recalled his encouragement and support when he was able to show it. I can still breathe in his strength and love.

Being a pack rat, I had love letters Frank had written to me over the years that I could refer back to whenever I needed a boost. I would look at his handwriting and the way he eloquently shared his love for me. Yes, reading them was a bittersweet experience, but comforting none the less. Once I penned a letter from him after he died. I knew him well enough to surmise the advice, wisdom, and words of encouragement he would say if he could. It was a letter from my 6 foot 6-inch angel in the form of a linebacker with very large and impressive wings.

I also had a beautiful experience with my mother after she died. It was my fiftieth birthday and I was longing for her presence. She died six years prior to my special birthday. I went into a meditation and all of a sudden I felt her. When I was a small child she began scratching my head and I loved it. We continued this until the last time I visited her. I would sit on the floor at her feet, lean my head on her knee, and she would lovingly scratch away. In my meditation, all of a sudden, I felt my head being scratched like only my mom could do it. It was an amazing realization and it ushered floods of happy tears. It has been the only time I have felt anything tangible with her since she died. What a fabulous birthday present.

Dreams

It is quite common to have dreams of your loved one once they pass. I have had some interesting dreams concerning Frank since his death. Some of the dreams seemed to be like normal dreams, but some were different. They seemed like I pierced the veil of death. I would wake and know I had been with Frank. In one such dream, we touched the tips of our index fingers together like we did in life to say I love you. I woke with a start when it happened in the dream state.

Another night I again awoke suddenly. I had been with Frank and we were looking deeply into each other's eyes, touching, and beginning to make love. At that point I thought, *This isn't a dream. We are really touching through the veil of death*, and with that thought I woke up. It was very powerful, a gift. I kept trying to go back and the next time I promised not to think but just feel.

Two years after his death he came to me in the dream state to kiss me even though we both knew he had died. He could give me a gentle surface kiss. He wanted to try a more penetrating kiss but couldn't. It was a strange sensation and it felt real, more than a dream as I reflected back on it the next morning.

Around the same time I dreamt that he had one hand amputated. It was raw and bleeding. He then cut off his other hand. He couldn't do anything without his hands. I didn't understand why he cut it off. When I shared the dream with my counselor she said that he no longer has a "hands-on" relationship with me.

On the night of the second anniversary of Frank's death, or graduation as I often refer to it, I had a dream of Frank. A woman asked him if he would be there to help her in life. He said, "As long as you need me, I will be here." I knew this was my subconscious reassuring me that he was still there for me.

I have had several dreams where I am with Frank and then all of a sudden I realize that it is a dream and in reality he is dead, and I wake up immediately. I believe these dreams were showing me that my psyche was integrating the truth of his death that took such a long time to absorb. I have heard that there is no resistance when we are sleeping and thus it is easier to make contact with our loved ones in the non-physical world.

I realize that all the times I have heard Frank or consciously connected with him or my mother, or have had spiritual visions of any type, I am in a non-resistant state and have a feeling of well-being. I have been deeply relaxed through massage, energy work, meditation, and surrender. You might or might not have such experiences, but they are possible when you let go and move into a peaceful state.

A woman shared with me that her father who had died appears in her dreams when she is in need of support and encouragement. She describes these experiences as seeming real rather than a mere dream.

A friend of mine shared some interesting dream experiences she had after her son died in a tragic skydiving accident when his parachute didn't open. She knew he had died before she was told. She knew as soon as she heard he had gone to jump that day that he was going to die. She tried to call him to beg him not to go and couldn't reach him. For six months after he died she connected with him at night through her dreams. He was in the dark, miserable and wanting to come back. She encouraged him to look for the light. Finally, he said he found it and his grandmother was waiting in a beautiful glow. He showed his mother what he saw. He said later he was working with children who had just died. He took her to the children and she knew by looking at each child how they had died. Her son was happy, but still wanted to return to the earth. One night he told her he was coming back to the earth and their contact ceased after that. Four years later in a dream, she found herself in a tenement in a ghetto home. There was a four-year-old boy with his little sister. The dad was a loving, caring, warm, and gentle man. My friend knew that the boy was her lost son. She even recognized his hands and she now has such peace. She felt that she was able to peer into his world and knew his new dad would care for him.

Honoring Your Loved One

Remember the traits you appreciated in your loved one. Write them down. Now think of ways to emulate those qualities in your life. I decided to let Frank's greatest strengths live through me and be a monument to my love for him. I often say and believe that he helped create the person I am today. It felt so good to list his beautiful attributes.

I also made other lists concerning Frank. I recalled things that we shared that were funny. I wrote about my most cherished memories of him as well. I compiled a sheet of teachings he taught through example by observing how he lived his life and uplifted others. I gathered all the lovely things people said about my husband and how they will remember him.

Paula, a friend of mine, shared that after her husband died, she created a painting depicting him in symbols and images. It didn't include a picture of his face. She used mixed media, combining materials from his shirts, paint, and a metal pin of a bear that he often wore which was his totem animal. She also had special words incorporated into the design. It was a lovely tribute to him.

One man I met fashioned a small shrine to his late wife. It had a small photo of her, some small things that she had cherished, a tiny vase with a flower, and a candle. They were assembled on a shelf on a wall in his living room. Each night at a set time he lit the candle.

Recently I read online about a ninety-one-year-old man who lost his wife after seventy-five years of marriage. About a month after she died he wrote her a song, "Sweet Loraine." He entered it in a contest and won. His song of tribute is now recorded.

I kept squares of material from Frank's favorite shirts or ones I loved seeing on him. These became a small quilted throw that I could wrap around me like a giant hug, a comforting comforter if you will. I had intended to embroider phrases and symbols on the quilt, but never got around to doing it. I could have also added actual photos printed on material and stitched them into the mosaic.

I found a special way to honor Frank. He loved wolves. I ordered a wolf sponsorship for my niece's elementary school in his memory. The school's mascot was the wolf so this felt so perfect to do. The school was able to choose which wolf they wanted to sponsor, received a newsletter, and they were sent educational materials about wolves. I cried when I thought of the idea knowing how right it was.

By concentrating on these positive memories, traits, and projects, your mind is led away from the negative memories of your loved one's death. Nothing can take these precious souvenirs away from you.

I wrote in my journal:

> *Today at the hospice support session I shared how I feel Frank's strength inside me, supporting me. I also shared that I'm learning not to cling to the way our relationship was, but I am working to accept the new form and be fed by it. I am who I am because he loved me. He continues to give me love and such inner strength.*

I shared these words in one of the letters I wrote to Frank: "Our love knows no boundaries; nothing divides our oneness, not even death!" Years after Frank died, I can say we still have a relationship, even though it is much different than when he was here in physical form. I still feel his strength, support, and amazing love.

Relating to Yourself

During your intrepid odyssey of grief you will not always recognize yourself as you enter your own dark continent within. You are going through major transitions and transformation. You will need blessings of understanding, compassion, love, and patience from yourself, as well as others. It is a good idea to befriend yourself as you morph into this new identity. I decided to court this new being that was evolving. I wanted to take care of myself as Frank would if he saw me in such a raw and fragile state. I knew my shattered heart needed tender and attentive care. I decided to take on the voyage of discovery, a quest of the emerging me. I discovered by losing myself in grief I found a very true and authentic self and I ultimately became my best friend. This didn't happen quickly by any means. At times I definitely didn't care for this new me during the process, which was rather like the larvae stage for a butterfly – not pretty. In this process you might need to plumb the depth and breadth of your being as I did before you make it to the other side. I did a lot of floundering before I got anywhere near surviving or had flourishing as a possibility on my radar. My being needed time to process as I emptied all my sorrow.

"What is the agent of that definitive transformation? Nothing less than death. God must make room for Himself in us, hollowing us out and emptying us, if he is finally to penetrate us. The function of death is to provide the necessary entrance into our inmost selves. O God, grant that I may understand that it is you who are painfully parting the fibers of my being in order to penetrate the very marrow of my substance." ~ Tielhard de Chardin

A year after Frank was gone, I sat by Josie, a vibrant older woman, on a flight from England back to the States. We had a stimulating conversation. Earlier in her life she went through the difficulties of a divorce and she shared that she had more sadness over not knowing herself. After the separation she realized she didn't know what she liked, what she wanted, or who she was. She said that after she learned who she was, the right man came into her life. She not only cultivated self-knowledge, but it resulted in self-love.

We can come to understand ourselves in the valleys of life. **Often it takes being on our own to experience intimate solitude where true awareness can blossom.** Here we can meet our authentic selves and hear our inner wisdom and guidance. So often we associate being on our own as being lonely. Solitude doesn't need to be a negative state to be avoided. We are so afraid to be alone that we fill our lives with noise, computers, television, cell phones, or anything that provides a distraction from our thoughts. When we are forced to be on our own, we are lost; we don't know ourselves and we do anything to frantically fill that vacuum. It is wise to learn to be comfortable with your own company. When Frank died, I had never lived on my own, but I had learned to be at ease when solitary. In solitude, I become whole and reconnect with my inner core, my inner wisdom, and my inner wellspring of hope. In stillness you feed your soul. If you find you have desert wastes in your heart and are a stranger to yourself, one answer is to go within. For me, in the times that I have plummeted the lowest I have always had a driving need to seek solitude, to replenish and rebuild from within. I knew it was temporary and necessary. I don't mean I had to be constantly alone, but I protected large chunks of time for just me. It was a survival strategy rather than adding more distracting activities. These centrifugal distractions throw us more off balance rather than bringing us to a still point center.

My mother would occasionally declare an "emotional health day" for me when I was a child. She would have me stay home from school, not for a physical illness but because I was spinning with so much on my plate. She knew the importance of creating a space for solace in stillness. In that space I learned to transform overwhelm into balance. I called on my mother's wise teaching when Frank died and knew it was necessary for me to cocoon to restore my equilibrium. I knew for sure I needed more than one "emotional health day" to cope with the spin I was in then!

I knew I needed time and space to reprioritize my life and to turn within to see what I needed. Some might not understand your needs, but you need to voice them anyway. I didn't care if others understood or not and neither should you. Your true friends will support you. **Now is the time to be your own best friend.** Stay conscious throughout your process.

I felt so many of my boundaries dissolve with the trauma of loss. I felt so raw in my vulnerability. I knew I needed to protect myself. I sensed the last thing I needed was to be in a large group or even go to a mall. If I made a plan, before it happened I would check with my inner self to make sure it still was the right plan for me. I honored my rhythm and my current state of being. I would try to determine daily my inner weather report. For example, how was I breathing? How was I feeling? What were my thoughts doing for or to me and how present was I at the time? I made a point to monitor my television time and I also watched very closely the amount of alcohol I consumed. Not wanting to avoid my mourning, I was careful not to do anything that could be destructive. I absolutely didn't want to go lower than I already was. Of course, I wasn't always successful with these intentions. If I observed something I wasn't happy with I tried not to berate myself. An airplane on automatic pilot doesn't stay exactly on course: it deviates and then realigns over and over. It is not static; it goes off and then comes back to center. Feeling lost will be normal. Feeling lost reminds me of a time after Frank died when I was driving alone in France and going in circles on a roundabout. I didn't know which exit to take, so I kept circling. A thought jumped into my head, *No one in the world knows where I am, not even me!* I burst into laughter. The same applies to your unique mourning path. Don't give up on yourself even if at times it feels like you are going in circles.

One thing I did to bring myself back to center was an exercise I had used as a management consultant. I made a list of my best traits, strengths, or best qualities. I brainstormed and then distilled them down to the top six. I looked to my past and what others had said to me about the type of person I was. I wrote: joyful, creative, enthusiastic, inspiring, loving, communicative, and spiritual. I put the list where I could see it every day. It reminded me that even though I didn't feel I was currently demonstrating a particular attribute, the trait was still inside me. Realizing some of them had been on the back burner since Frank's death, I set the intention to demonstrate one of my strengths per week. I was determined not to let my best assets die along with Frank. I suggest you make a similar commitment.

In the hospice support group we discussed our changing identities. As we talked, I sketched a wagon wheel-type model. I put my six strengths in the center with spokes coming off for the different roles I filled at the time. It was strange not to have a spoke for the role of wife; it had been a big piece of my vision of myself and for some it was their whole identity. Your true identity is that center hub that expresses into your various roles. You have to believe that your true self will shine forth again. Trust your inner gyroscope to kick in and guide you back on track towards you. Part of your changing description is because of new roles and skills you were forced to pick up. I was expanding and had many growing edges. I learned about taxes, paying the bills, computers, and settling an estate for a start. It often felt like forced growth in a hothouse called grief. I prayed that all the growing pains wouldn't be for naught.

"Out of suffering have emerged the strongest souls; the most massive characters are seared with scars." ~ Kahlil Gibran

Celebrate each and every piece of progress you achieve. Acknowledge every step and every scar as you heal.

Engaging with Life

Your thoughts about and connection to life might have been abruptly changed when your loved one died. You might not even be aware of the shifts. I knew I didn't care if I were here on earth or not when I was on a flight from the UK two months after Frank's death. The plane lost one of its two engines and had to return to Heathrow. The other passengers were terrified as we heard a loud and strange sound: I didn't care what happened to me as I watched fuel drain from one of the wings. I figured if we crashed I would be with Frank.

A few months later, I received an energy session with Peter Hurley, a colleague and teacher of mine. During the session as he worked on me I heard from deep inside me the words, *I want to live!* When I told Peter after the work, he said he got several times that I didn't want to be here subconsciously. He said I needed to recommit more deeply to my role on earth and added that I had a conflict about being here; it was like I was committing a slow suicide.

I later wrote in my journal:

> *I recall last year talking to God, before we knew of Frank's illness. I said I would go anywhere, do anything He wanted, but please don't ask me to give up Frank. Now I must accept this tremendous loss. As I think back about the session with Peter, I realize I have only been half-ass living. I have been going through the motions of living, but my real spirit isn't here. I know I must try to really live with more passion and enthusiasm. I didn't even realize I didn't want to be here. I suppose just being aware of my state of mind is good. Now I can work with it consciously. I do want to live for both myself and Frank. He would want me to go on in typical Gail fashion, not like a zombie. I would want the same for him, if I had been the one to die. He died, I didn't! I can't quit living at fifty-one, although the thought of a long life without him is unbearable to think about. I will take it one day at a time. I will develop a ritual of commitment to life and to birth more of my consciousness.*

Peter mentioned a slow unconscious suicide. If you have any thoughts of actual suicide, promise me and your loved one that you will immediately reach out for help. Call a suicide hotline, your doctor, a therapist, a clergyman, a friend or anyone who can help you—right now.

Later in my journal I wrote:

> *A new life is calling, imploring me to let go, release my grip on the past, and break out of my self-imposed cocoon. I need to connect to the fluidity of life, the flow. I must first let go of my firm grip, my need to control. I must choose to go forward with courage. I remind myself how Frank was able to stay in that*

flow until the end. Just four days before he died, I awoke to give him his final meds of the night. I opened my eyes and Frank was facing me in the hospital bed beside me. He had a huge grin wrapped around his face. I asked what he was smiling about as he was paralyzed from the waist down and blind, to list a few of his many symptoms. He cheerfully responded, "I'm smiling because I'm just so happy to be here and I've been watching you sleep and you are so beautiful." He quickly added, "And I'm not just saying that because I can't see." I loved how we both laughed. Frank faced death with such presence, grace, and courage and kept living until his last breath. He taught me that grace is a vibrant relationship with life. If he could do that, I can commit to doing the same. I can try.

Heartfelt Suggestions ⟶

Now it is time to go to a quiet place where you can have some time with yourself. Bring a pen and notebook. Place your hand over your heart and close your eyes. Take several slow deep breaths down into your lower belly. Allow your breath to guide you to the peaceful place within your heart. Now open your eyes and begin reading and reflect on the suggestions. Remember this is part of your conscious mourning and it is sacred work.

1. What kind of experiences, dreams, and thoughts show you still have a relationship with your loved one after their death? Do you ever feel their presence? Have you written them a letter?

2. Are you doing anything to honor your loved one? What can you do to remember them? Is there anything you could write, create or do?

3. What traits of your loved one can you emulate, express?

4. What funny memories do you want to keep?

5. What are your most cherished memories of them?

6. What lovely things have people shared about your lost one?

7. What good things did your loved one teach by example?

8. Have you been writing down your feelings and thoughts?

9. What kind of friend are you being for yourself?

10. Do you recognize yourself in grief?

11. Do you have the desire to cocoon, to isolate? Are you balancing some time with others as well?

12. Are you comfortable with solitude?

13. Create a list of your best traits, strengths or qualities by brainstorming. Now distill down to your top six.

14. What is your current relationship to life? Do you need to recommit to life?

CHAPTER FOUR

RELEASING: Embrace and Express

WHEN YOU ARE PLUNGED INTO GRIEF, you are entangled in foreign emotions while unbearable thoughts tie you in knots. How do you purge yourself of extreme feelings and the incessant mind chatter? How do you go the distance in your heart without hardening it? How do you cope with the vulnerability, the fragility, the rawness, and the extreme suffering? Your natural reaction is to protect yourself from the pain and close down. At the beginning of my mourning journey I wrote in my journal:

> *I think of our cat Rumi when we got him, and how when he went outside for the first time he was terrified and overwhelmed. He would go a little distance and run back to us, the familiar. As I open my heart to such pain, I want to retreat and close down. I, too, want the familiar, but it is gone. I need to learn to relax within the moment whether it is painful or joyful. I often feel overwhelmed and afraid like Rumi. I must learn to lean into my pain and let it flow through me and out.*

What you avoid won't go away and results in suffering which will eventually surface. For example, think of trying to keep a rubber ball under water. The more you struggle to hold it beneath the surface, the stronger it returns with even greater force. Grief is also strenuous and trying to push it down zaps more of your energy. Clinging to your past and trying in fear to push away your future doesn't work. It doesn't allow you to experience the present—the place of power. You need to face your grief head-on and release it. Release means to set free. In this chapter I will discuss how grief affects you physically, emotionally, and mentally. It can feel at times like you are living in a thick fog or cloud. Often it is tough to have clarity or vision. I wondered at times, *What am I feeling? Where am I? How will I get past this? Where am I going?* I will offer suggestions and tools to help you gain clarity and equilibrium. I aim to empower you and offer some guidance. Yes, this is a heroic journey, but you can do this. You might even ultimately lend poignancy to your pain, see some relevance, perhaps some teaching, or make a reaffirmation of life. You can find yourself and your way. Keep walking. Take one step at a time.

Tears: "Mourning" Dew

One of the first and most obvious releases I experienced, and you might as well, was crying. In the beginning it was difficult for me to really let go and sob without holding myself back. I had to be strong while my husband was ill and at that time I didn't allow myself to let go very often. But when he died my tears burst their dam and for a long time I wondered if I would ever stop weeping.

Sorrow Sojourn
The Naked Tears of Grief

Why is it that you well up and tears stream down your face? Weeping is a normal human response to intense life experiences. Crying indicates a literal overflow of emotions, a "fountain" of feelings, if you will. The birth of a child can move you to tears of joy. Saying good-bye to a friend or family member after a visit can cause tears to spring forth. Movies, a sentimental TV show, or a book can touch you deeply at a heart level and trigger a waterfall of tears. What about those Hallmark card moments? You can even laugh so hard that tears stream down your face and your stomach aches. Any kind of loss or tragedy can be accompanied by grief and often tears are a part of that process, but a major catalyst is the loss of a loved one through death.

It's important to remember when the tears begin to not stop them. Open the floodgate and let the dammed-up feelings flow. At first you might be very uncomfortable letting yourself go. You might try to stifle the tears by forcefully exhaling, clearing your throat, saying or thinking to yourself, *Don't lose control. Get a grip. Don't be a crybaby.* Try to think of the tears like steam that rises to release the pressure from a pot of boiling water. They are really a gift and I consider them sacred. The flow may be sparked sometimes by surprising things: the lyrics in a song, something you see, or words you hear. The triggers for the seemingly endless waterworks are all true blessings that will heal you.

Tears bathe your emotional body like a shower cleanses the physical. The element of water is associated with emotions and the emotional body needs to be fluid. Energy needs to flow like water throughout your being. In the energy work I do I know that the blockage of energy due to stuck or stagnant emotions can cause you problems. The shedding of tears can break down such a block. Understanding this helped me to allow the flood of tears to fall rather than stifle them. There are actually crying clubs in Japan where people gather to cry. Sad music is played or a sad film shown. One person begins to cry, then another, and another. Some cultures consider it shameful to cry in public, so they will do it in private with others, men and women alike.

The United Kingdom has crying clubs now. Though there may be times or places that crying might be inappropriate, I say that there are times that it would be inappropriate *not* to express your sadness at the loss of your loved one.

It is much more authentic to react normally to the grieving process, like a small child who emotes freely. About a week after Frank died, my dear sister insisted we go to the movies. At the end of the film it hit me that I wanted my life to be a film that I could walk out of. That triggered complete sobbing. My patient sis just sat it out. She knew I needed to do this to release some of the strong and painful emotions I was holding within. Meanwhile everyone left the theatre and people began streaming in for the next showing. When I finally became aware again of where I was, I realized there was a giant circle of empty seats around us. I am sure all were wondering what kind of movie they were about to watch that elicited such a response. I do feel it is important to find ways to honor your true feelings and to express them. At times of extreme pain and vulnerability, if you can't take off the masks of societal programming, when can you?

If you feel your tears should be private, fine, but allow your tears to flow. Dammed-up streams become very stagnant and unhealthy. I found it good to have someone to cry with who wouldn't stop me with words like, "Everything will be all right. Don't cry. Let's dry your tears," or try to divert you with another activity.

At the website www.EmotionalProcessing.org.uk/tears I found this quote regarding a study of crying: "Randolph Cornelius (1986) systematically analyzed the content of popular articles on weeping in the press from 1850 to 1985 and found a major theme was that crying was considered an important means of releasing physiological tensions; if it wasn't released, it would find an outlet in some other way, such as affecting the person's body and possibly causing disease. 94% of the articles recommended letting tears flow."

I personally feel emotional tears can include happy tears and sad tears. I am quickly moved to happy tears when I feel tremendous joy or breathe in great beauty, perhaps from an incredible landscape. A year after Frank's passing, I became so excited when I finally wept happy tears again. It happened while I was receiving energy work. I felt such a sense of being blessed that streams of happy tears flowed.

In William H. Frey's book *Crying: The Mystery of Tears,* I learned that happy tears are basically salt water. Sad tears contain the same chemicals and enzymes that are found in tumors, ulcers, other lumps, and sicknesses in the body. Crying flushes out these toxic chemicals that accumulate and are part of the sadness and heartache experience.

From my journal:

> *In the Breath class this week, Holland, the teacher, read a passage about being in the void. As she read, my tears trickled down my face. In the place of emptiness and disconnectedness, being so vulnerable is a door to other states of consciousness. She read that aloneness sets the stage, and in silence our inner companions can now be heard. We feel raw, vulnerable, and are strangers in a new land... Amen. That is exactly what I feel. She read on that just being can be magical, if not pressured to move on. This is a very alone state. It is like exhaling and really letting go completely. Like the trapeze act where you let go of one trapeze, swing and soar through space trusting another trapeze will meet you and you'll know the time to grab for it—but not too soon. This really resonated with me and moved me deeply. I was already feeling a lot. Rumi, my cat, didn't come home last*

night. This is the first time he didn't in the nine months he has lived with me. I didn't sleep well, checking at the door every couple of hours and worrying. I figured finally he would show up for his breakfast. No show. I began to fear he would be gone, too, that I would lose him like Frank. Luckily, just before I needed to leave for class he arrived home. I decided to meditate since I was in such a state. This was the first time I had meditated in over eight months, since Frank's illness began. This was good— touching home base again. Peace flooded my being as I went off to class. Today I was the client and being coached in breathing. I need to breathe more fully into my spine, into the front and back of my body as well as my abdomen and chest. I chose to focus on the apparent energy block in my throat and jaw and to align my energy bodies. As we worked, it felt like a hand pressing on my chest. She wasn't doing it. Then I began coughing a lot, releasing, and then I switched to crying and it quickly escalated into sobbing. I asked silently "What is this?" and I knew I was releasing the fear of losing Frank before he died. That was my biggest fear during that period. Rumi helped me to get in touch with it. It all was so beautifully orchestrated. Holland joined in and had me open my eyes and look into hers and breathe with her. It was good for me to let go and sob. I don't sob very often. The counselor in Santa Cruz said I needed to let go.

I learned through the *Growing Through Loss* course that some people prefer not to be touched when crying. Not me. I wanted and needed physical touch more than ever. I guess the best thing is to ask someone who is crying if they want a hug. My instinct before losing Frank would have been to immediately reach out to someone who was upset. I am learning how to better support others through my own experiences. I also don't mind asking for a hug when I need it now. Tell people if you would like to be touched or not when you are crying. Your needs can change, so witness what you feel you require in that moment. Voice your needs and desires. People can't read your mind.

From my journal at about seven months into grief:

> I went shopping this week for a special bottle to collect my tears. They are sacred tears that I will allow to spill from my inner being. I won't stifle them. Later in the week I received a newsletter from one of my students. Katherine Rosengren wrote the following untitled poem:
>
> I leap.
> Will my wings open?
> My heart speaks of tears
> They cleanse my soul
> They heal wounds
> In Turkey they are collected and saved
> in little bottles of mouth blown glass
> to preserve the sacred tears of mourners.
> Why do you weep?
> Why do you hide your tears from me?
> Eyes are the portals to the soul
> They weep
> Tears trickle down our throats and backs in
> Tiny rivers
> I want to know why you weep,
> And why you hide your tears from me?

I hadn't heard about collecting the tears when I decided to gather them. I called Katherine and told her of the synchronicity of my action and her poem. I was getting a lot of confirmation for what I was doing and thinking. I have since learned that in both Rome and ancient Greece, tears were collected during bereavement, and I have seen some of these exquisitely beautiful vessels of love in museums. Psalm 56:8 says "You have collected all my tears and preserved them in Thy bottle! You have recorded every one in your book." So God thinks our tears are sacred, too. More research revealed that a tear bottle is called a *lachrymal*. They were used in the Victorian era, or nineteenth century, and have been referred to as Victorian tear catchers, usually used by widowed brides on the day of the funeral. The bride would collect all the tears she cried on that day and during the first year after her husband's death. The vial was worn around her neck and on the first anniversary of his death she poured the preserved tears atop the gravesite. Another source explained that the mourning period would end when the tears evaporated in the vial. In some remote areas of Turkey they still make tear vessels of pottery and the collected drops are poured on a tree or flower that has been planted in memory of their lost loved one.

I received a synchronistic gift as I was proofreading this manuscript for the publisher. Paula, a friend who didn't know about me writing about tear vessels, gave me one to celebrate this book. She wondered if I would know what it was.

November 23rd, seven months after loss, journal entry:

> *I had an energy session with Peter today. I told him about my glass container to collect my sacred tears. He suggested I make a homeopathic remedy. I can take my own tears as the basis and dilute them with water and percussion the mix. I will try it. I was listening to music today and heard the words sung by Sarah McLachlan in her song Fumbling Towards Ecstasy: "If I shed a tear I won't cage it. I won't fear love and if I feel a rage I won't deny it." I believe we can get direction or messages from all kinds of sources. Grief's grip is so strong. Tears are the dew of death or loss. Mourning dew, that's what my tears are. I want our souls to fly across the huge abyss and span the ethers. Let the portal of pain become the doorway, let love become the bridge. I don't weep for what might have been, I weep for the loss of what was. What was my biggest joy has left me in my greatest sorrow.*
>
> *Tears are the waters of the soul carving consciousness like a grand canyon. In my suffering, my pain, I also feel beauty and peace pulling together, uniting the dualities. It is an awesome experience, transcending sensations. It is difficult to describe. I know my tears are sacred and they are messengers of my deep love. Perhaps tears are the language of the soul.*

Tears may flow when we are touched deeply through direct experience or by being moved by someone else's story. One evening at a concert, I heard a woman singing a beautiful aria. It was the one I heard on Paros soon after Frank died, the song that had opened me to loving opera. It touched me deeply. I explained that to the singer after she sang. We both let the tears surface and cascade. Crying together can be a powerful dimension of interpersonal communication, a communion of souls. Crying with others also gives you comfort.

Journal entry:

> *Today I received an awesome bodywork session. I held the intention to allow or invite up any terror and shock from a year ago. I found I had stuffed a lot of terror in my derrière. I guess I just wanted to sit that one out! The more I got in touch with the terror, it changed to deep sadness. I sobbed and began weeping that sounded like lamenting. They were soul sobs. At times I sighed and sighed in a rhythm. There was quite a bit of pain again in my chest area. I had big coughing releases. I had to sit up and Paula did cupping on my back which released through more coughing. Three times both of us smelled something unusual. It seemed like anesthetic to me and she thought like moth balls. Both could be right. I was releasing things I had stored away or I had anesthetized not to feel. She got that it all had to do with survival issues and security. That sure fits with my dreams of insecurity lately. I know that the body is made up of at least 75% water. I have cried so much I should look like a prune. Maybe I do!*

After that experience of sighing in a rhythm I decided to learn more about laments. I found an interesting book, *Dangerous Voices – Women's Laments and Greek Literature* by Gail Holst-Washaft. Weeping and singing the pain into song is itself an externalizing of suffering. She explains like the cries that punctuate the text, so sobs, sighs, and sudden intakes of breath are integral to the performance of a lament. To go from private tears to shrill cries that affect the landscape all around is cathartic and helps to resolve an inner torment. Laments help reorder your inner emotional reaction to death. There is a need for ritual, to externalize the chaos and disorder. The form of lament is varied from an elaborate poem to tuneful weeping. In ancient Greece, professional mourners called moirologists performed choruses and wailing songs at funerals. A lament is an artistic composition inspired by bereavement or loss. They give vent to passionate feelings. Laments transform yours or another's pain into a work of art.

I think my attempts at poetry and listening to operas were my experience with laments. I have definitely had times of public display as well, in the grocery store, a movie theatre, etc. I think our society hampers open grieving and most people don't want to see the pain. I believe it must be expressed not repressed; it should be honored. Men in particular are raised to not show their tears. I believe that strong men can cry. If you were taught to suck it up and not show your true emotions, you can rewrite that script to a healthier scenario. Rewrite that right now. The University of Pittsburgh School of Nursing did a study and showed that healthy people cry more freely and more frequently.

Tears create rainbows in your soul. I did a sketch of a swirling rainbow with tears spraying from the center. Rainbows are seen after stormy weather and they symbolize hope which I clung to during my grieving.

During Holy week in Greece there is a lovely church service in the late evening on Good Friday. At one point in the ceremony thousands of rose petals are dropped from the high dome onto the Christ casket in a breathtaking cascade. I tune in to the personal grief of Mary Magdalene and Mother Mary and I liken the rose petals with tears falling in grief. This ritual has always moved me as the colorful petals rain down and hundreds of candles are glowing. The priest says that the two Mary's scatter rose petals on Christ's tomb. Your tears are sacred. Your grief work is sacred!

There are definitely times when it is very appropriate to cry and a time of great loss is one of those times.

When Shari, the volunteer hospice coordinator, asked how I was doing in my mourning process, I gave her an update. She handed me a card which she had pinned to her note board that said, "Grief is like weather. In the beginning there are torrents of rain and buffeting. Then the rain is more intermittent and there are long periods of drought. Then all of a sudden there is a flash flood. As time goes by there will be an occasional rain storm. Then there will be days of drizzle." I was in the drizzle period when I read that card, but then a flash flood would come at any time. I cried with Shari as we spoke; her son had died several years before, so she understood grief firsthand.

Tears are not a sign of weakness, but rather a mark of strength.

Heartfelt Suggestions

Now it is time to go to a quiet place where you can take some time for yourself. Bring a notebook and pen. Place your hand over your heart and close your eyes. Take several slow deep breaths down into your lower belly. Allow your breath to guide you to the peaceful place within your heart. Now open your eyes and begin reading and reflect on the suggestions. Remember this is part of your conscious mourning and it is sacred work.

1. How comfortable are you with crying?

2. Can you cry only when alone?

3. When you do cry, do you try to stifle the tears?

4. What is your reaction when someone else is crying?

5. What could you do to help release any pent-up tears?

Remember they can help you to heal by releasing the pain of grief. Some suggestions: music that stirs you, movies that might prompt tears to flow or a book that moves you.

6. Make a list of things that have moved you to happy tears during your life.

Emotions

The shadows of grief are often emotions that are battering you like a tsunami does a shoreline. According to Wikipedia, the word emotion dates back to 1579. It is adapted from a French word *emouvoir* meaning "to stir up." They can stir you to joy or despair.

Emotional pain signals that you are out of balance—surprise, surprise! Frank's death triggered the most intense chaotic emotions of my life. My feelings completely ran amok. I often felt like I was drowning in a deep sea of emotions without direction or any bearings. I needed a GPS for my life. I had emotional whiplash as they ran the full gamut ricocheting through my being and life. They were also huge, bigger than 3D feelings. They were surrealistic, like I was living in a Salvador Dali painting. They left me feeling battered and broken. Emotions can be more exhausting than physical labor.

I speak of the struggle and energy it takes to squelch difficult feelings. Restricted emotions can also result in physical symptoms: low energy, stomach issues, breathing problems, swallowing difficulties, and disturbed sleep, for example. Please don't fall into the trap of thinking that the miserable feeling will go away if you ignore it. It is wiser to acknowledge the existence of your intense and deep feelings, and learn to express them in constructive, safe, and perhaps creative ways. It does take courage to delve into the raw, pure emotions as they break over and through you. You can't stop a wave, but you can learn to surf it. You can also decide which wave to hold onto and which one to let pass by.

There is something very interesting about blocking an emotion: you can't selectively block just one emotion without blocking them all. Shut down fear and you shut down joy, excitement, and every other emotion. Bury them all and you flatline emotionally. You are numb. You are actually slowing down your vibration, inhibiting the flow of your life force, until you are like the walking dead. You might think that certain emotions aren't spiritual or they are improper, so you deny their existence. When you do that, the emotion can get stuck in your body, creating an energy blockage which can stop vibrating completely. When you suppress, you clog your body. Most illnesses have an emotional component.

You need to find life-enhancing ways to deal with your passionate emotions. Release your grip, welcome all your feelings, and allow them to flow through you without resistance. Emotions are energy and flow is a key concept: don't hold bitterness, anger, or the like, in your heart. These unresolved emotions can build a wall around your heart and down the flow of your life force. Think twice about carrying this type of baggage throughout your life. Whatever you carry, you live with daily. I think of permitting my feelings to flow like they are a freely running river. Let the tears cascade without resistance. Cradle the emotion within acceptance. Don't sidestep the abyss; ALLOW the feelings. When you are consciously choosing to allow the emotion, you are in control, not the emotion. Note that when you observe your feeling and choose to ride it, that you are in a powerful witness state: your *Resilient Heart*®.

Can you tell what you are feeling? As a child I wasn't allowed to even say I was angry. I learned to deny that emotion and often would call it hurt. It was okay for me to be hurt but not angry. I wasn't allowed the "D" word either: depressed. So I was operating with a limited palette of emotions. I have since decided I want a complete palette, a full range of the spectrum available to me. A full life lives the full spectrum. A feeling is neither right nor wrong. It is how we express it that can be healthy or destructive. During my mourning it was a huge risk to be so raw and authentic as I expressed the incredibly intense emotions. I was way out of my comfort zone, emotionally naked, but it would have been a greater hazard for me to have played it safe and risked nothing. To be free of the pain I had to risk being transparent with myself and others.

I had the goal or intention to be current in my emotions well before Frank died. By that I mean, if I get angry today, it is only about what happened today. If I still hold unprocessed feelings of anger and something triggers my anger today, my reaction might be way over the top for what just occurred. I don't want to operate like a volcano that spews out old pent up emotions. As I was grieving I wanted to honor all the old repressed feelings I had squirreled away. I invited them to surface as I was broken open anyway.

Just before Frank was ill I processed old grief around moving so much in my life. I have lived in fifteen states and attended twenty-five schools and universities. No, I didn't get kicked out of a lot of the schools as one friend suggested. Yes, I was a military brat – Air Force. I had said goodbye many times to many people and places. The repressed grief erupted when I moved yet again just before Frank got sick. I am so glad I did that process before my huge loss. I believe as an old grief is released there is more room for joy to enter. I didn't feel great joy for quite a long time, but I did begin to feel lighter.

By allowing the movement, the flow of your feelings, you can transform your shattered heart and observe alchemy happening within. Your wide open and bleeding heart will become a *Resilient Heart*®. Feelings are the pathway and the software of your soul. You can't heal when you are unable to feel. It takes strong determination to ride the emotion when a strong one rips through you. **Feelings will course through your being much faster without resistance.** What you resist persists. To live through the pain, be transformed by it, and then transform others by it, is to become the hero.

Many people mask their pain with addictions. Some of the main addictions people turn to are alcohol, food, shopping, sex, and work. I could definitely see how much easier it would be to mask the awful pain. Such addictions are distractions that take you away from processing and ultimately transforming your pain. I was determined to stay conscious and focused on my grief journey. I attempted to observe my behaviors and redirect myself if they weren't life enhancing or if they were a means of distraction. I often found myself off course and needed to bring myself back to my feelings to allow them to flow freely rather than avoiding them. I like the taste of alcohol so I was particularly mindful of drinking alone and how much I drank. What distractions do you tend to use to avoid feeling?

You might be tempted to turn to unhealthy ways of soothing yourself but there are healthy ways to self-soothe. You could try a warm bath, change your sheets, take a walk or a nap, get yourself some flowers, read something uplifting or try playing with a child or animal. I made a list of things that had made me feel good in my past. I noticed hardly anything on my list cost much money. I had things like drinking my coffee or tea out of a lovely china cup. I suggest you make such a list of things that feed your soul, so when you are tempted to comfort yourself with something unhealthy you can go to your list and choose something that is more appropriate for the moment.

I caution you that there is a difference in allowing an emotion to flow and clinging to it for dear life. Clinging to a disruptive feeling is choosing misery. Remember the idea is to let it flow through and out. Pay attention; notice that the more you feed an upsetting emotion, the stronger it gets and the charge increases. Also notice it increases by some thought you are repeating. When I practice bodywork I have you tell me what you have been feeling and thinking lately. If there is something with a big charge, I have you tune within and see where it has a corresponding sensation in your body. If you keep looking, you will find the place. Then breathe into that place with slow conscious breaths. If your thoughts stray from the place and your breathing, gently bring yourself back to the task. Sometimes it helps to place your hand on the spot if that is comfortable for you to do. After a bit, the charge on the emotion decreases or leaves completely. You can't be more in the present than when you are aware of your breathing. Feelings can be the gateway to being in the now.

I suggest being child-like. Children are authentic with their emotions. They express them and move on quite quickly. They aren't bothered with resistance; they allow freely and stay with it until it flows. Put down your defenses and let yourself be vulnerable and raw. Now, I am realistic and realize you can't always express your innermost feelings if you are at work or some other inappropriate place. Then it is good to create time and space where and when you can effectively release your emotions and express your various feelings.

Breathe into your feeling and observe where it is hanging out in your body until it shifts or moves. I want to discuss some other ways to deal with your emotions. Exercise is a great way to keep them moving. What can you do to make sure you are getting some kind of exercise? Health pioneer, Christine Northrup, M.D., expresses the importance of moving your emotions. "Tears, movement and sound are part of your emotional digestive system. They help release blocked energy in the body. Moving through pain by feeling your way through it is the pain that ends pain."

Emotions are associated with the element of water and ideally they are fluid. Getting into water helps clear your emotional body. A shower is ideal or a bath after a quick shower to calm you. Drinking water helps as well. Your brain functions clearer when hydrated. Most of us are a bit dehydrated in general. If you need to make a decision or take an exam, drink lots of water. As I cried so much, I needed to replenish a lot of fluids.

Journal Writing

Another way to cope and process strong emotions is to express them or give them a voice. What this does is externalize your pain and moves the stuck feeling. I found that when I spoke of my intense emotions I often got more clarity and affirmation of what was true for me. It connected my head and my heart. I shared in support groups and I shared with family and friends. I also wrote in journals. I hadn't kept one since I was a young girl except for holiday diaries. This was not a fun trip, but it certainly was a journey. I found that my journals became dear friends during my mourning process and brought me comfort.

I filled six notebooks during my grief journey. They held my most difficult and painful emotions: anguish, hostility, despair, my doubts, my confusion, terrors, frustrations, depression, and my loneliness. My slow return to the living was also documented as my growth and resilience began to seep to the surface. As I fought for my own survival, my journal notations were dispatches from the front lines of my grief experiences. My insights and moments of courage and conviction are documented. Writing helped me bring some clarity which I needed so desperately. When I read back to the first year I am astounded that I was so low, but at the same time I am proud that I pulled myself up out of that pit of despair.

I recommend you get a notebook and start to write down your feelings and thoughts if you aren't doing so already. I just used ordinary spiral bound notebooks. You can get a nicer journal if you'd like, but the point is to write and be comfortable doing it. Write in a private and relaxing location. Don't feel your writing must be perfect. Don't be concerned with punctuation, or grammar. No one is reading this but you unless you choose to share it with someone. I wrote at least several times per week. During some periods of my grief I wrote daily. But when you do write, keep at it long enough to release what is suppressed within you. You might start writing about one thing and it leads to something completely different. You can gain insight and touch on inner wisdom and guidance. You might think you are feeling one emotion, but when you write you learn there is a different underlying feeling. I gave an example where I first was feeling anger and then I realized underneath was a profound sadness. I would often begin writing by asking myself what I was feeling at the time and what thoughts were racing around my head. Some days a screaming emotion just spewed on the page as soon as I picked up a pen.

Here is such an example from my journal:

> This week is filled with fears and tears. I am feeling so anxious. I am paying bills and fears are leaping at me like flames. Will I run out of money? How can I make more? What will my future be like without Frank? Scary! The holidays are tough. I see all the lights going up that normally give me such joy. Christmas is about love and my love isn't here to share the season. I often watch other people living their lives and I am only an observer. I am a spectator and Frank and I always said life is not a spectator sport. I feel suspended. I wait for my real life, my old life to resume. I'm feeling overwhelmed with bills and the computer isn't working or the VCR. I need to find new tenants for my house in Greece. I just want to escape it all, the holidays and life. I feel lost; I don't know what to do with myself. It takes me so much longer to do things and they upset me when normally they wouldn't.

As you can see my emotions bounce and churn like a washing machine on the spin cycle. But it normally made me feel better just to write my feelings down. I thought of allowing my emotions to stream as I wrote.

I also poured out great memories of my beloved in my journals. Sometimes I added sketches and doodles to whatever I was expressing. My journals include letters to Frank as well. Later on my journey I added something I was grateful for daily. I tried my hand at poetry. I didn't care about the form being correct; that wasn't my intention. My purpose was to express what was going on inside of me, in order to ease pain and allow my bleeding heart a voice.

One of my poems:

Open to the Mystery

Have you emptied your core through grief my friend?
Have you known both laughter and loneliness?
Has your radiant heart expanded to experience
the total of life?
Your spirit is speaking; are you listening my friend,
listening to the wisdom that dwells within?
Do you drink from the well of your soul
and thirst no more?
Are you open to the mystery and the magic that life
delivers until the end?
Have you plumbed the exquisite depths
of your experiences
through tears of pain and joy?
Have you felt your heart explode with grief?
Have you risked your comfort zone to soar?
Let go, let go my friend, let resistance flow.
Your pain can be a doorway to treasures unknown.
Let go and LIVE!

Nature

Get into nature. Being in nature is very healing and helps calm you. As long as I can recall, going to the ocean has always brought me back into balance. For some it is going to the top of a mountain.

As a management consultant I helped people deal with stress. One of the coping techniques I suggested was getting into nature. It grounds you or balances you, leaving you much more stable. As a society we have gotten away from an intimate relationship with nature. After Frank died I knew I needed soil around me. I found a tiny apartment on the bottom floor of a house which had a sidewalk width of land along one wall. I put a lounge chair there and planted some flowers. Try to get into a garden or a city park. You can at least have an indoor plant. I am typing in a room full of orchids which I grow. Orchids have the highest energy frequency of any flower. Roses have the second highest, so it is very healing to have them around. For energy it is best if they are in pots or in the ground. Gardening is a great way to bring balance and grounding. Some days you might be tilling the soil and the next ripping weeds from the earth. Think how important it is to ground electricity. As you have intense emotions coursing through you, it is beneficial to ground yourself.

Walking barefoot on the earth is great, as is sitting on the ground with your back leaning on a tree. You guessed correctly; I have been seen hugging trees. I often add the intention that as I do these things I am breathing in balancing energy from the earth and I am exhaling the current strong emotion back into the ocean of energy to be recycled. Remember there is no bad energy – just stuck or stagnant energy that needs to move. Adding intention to what you are doing is bringing mindfulness to your actions. It is connecting to that inner observer, the wise part of you which always brings you into the present.

Meditation

As a consultant for stress management in corporations, I taught meditation under the guise of relaxation exercises before meditation was more widely accepted. It is an excellent way to befriend your Inner Wise One. It teaches you not to cling to any one feeling or thought. If you haven't tried it before it might be easier to do with an experienced person in meditation or use a recorded guided version. I first tried to do it in my 20s with little success, as I expected myself to be able to master it immediately.

I thought I had to rid my mind of all thoughts. I think that is nearly impossible now. I think the better approach is not to cling to a thought. Observe it and let it move on. It is easier when you decide what you *will* focus on. Your breath is a great focus. When you find your mind wandering, which it will, GENTLY bring your attention back to your breath. Think of walking with a small child on a path in nature. If the child wanders off the path you don't beat the child, you coax him back to the path. It doesn't matter how many times your mind wanders; the key is to realize it has and come back to the focus you have chosen. You might choose to concentrate on a concept like love or a candle flame. The benefits come from the process, not a specific goal; this really helps with stress.

Counseling is another way to process emotions. I had a month of counseling after Frank died and later in Santa Barbara I received Eye Movement Desensitization and Reprocessing (EMDR) work. EMDR focuses on troubled feelings, thoughts, physical sensations and behaviors. In the book *EMDR* by Francine Shapiro it explains that the process activates the person's innate ability to heal psychologically. You access memories but you don't dwell on them. It seemed to be a faster way of treatment than traditional counseling for me. It originally used eye movements. Patricia, my therapist, used music played through a headset which I wore. It would play in different ears creating changing patterns that balances the left and right brain hemispheres. This music brought me into a deep meditative state quickly. The book explained that it typically moves you into the present where you feel free and in control. I found that to be true for me. I was able to process and change the level of charge on many difficult and painful emotions in our weekly sessions. Usually we processed feelings around Frank's death and my life afterward, but sometimes we were led to some old emotion which we then processed. My inability to have children came up after so many years in a very powerful session resulting in a dramatic decrease of charge around the issue. If you opt for some form of counseling, find a therapist who you feel comfortable with. If you don't know of any, ask people who you respect for recommendations. If the first one doesn't feel like a good match for you, keep looking.

I now want to speak of a few specific emotions which seem common to most grievers.

Fear

Fear is the faith that things won't work out. I found the loss of my loved one triggered many fears. One was the fear of moving on after Frank's death. It was the concern that going forward in my life would distance me from him. I read that this concern often comes up if the relationship had been good. In a workshop I attended about losing a loved one, the speaker said at some point you need to relegate the relationship to your history. Her words stabbed me. I wrote that night in my journal:

> *I don't want to relegate you only to my past, my history! Frank, you will always be with me. You are a part of me and live in my heart. You helped create who I am.*

Years later, he isn't constantly part of my life, but he is present in many ways as I described in relating to your lost one. The relationship has just changed.

Another huge fear I wrestled with was about money. At times it would wake me up out of a sound sleep, and of course everything seems worse in the night. I decided I didn't want to live my life based on worry and fear. I never had and I didn't intend to start, but living that way was much more difficult than saying it. It really hit me when I saw myself struggling to buy a $7 tee shirt. I worked on this issue for several weeks using EMDR. I shared that I was struggling to have faith, and feeling like I had to do it all. I used the music with the headset while we did this work.

"Fear blocks you from your greatness and is also the doorway to it," Barbara Brennan said in her book, *Hands of Light.*

Near the first anniversary of Frank's death, strong fears surfaced around faith and money again. Long term renters were moving out of my home in Greece and I needed to do some work on it and find new renters. I didn't have the money to hire someone to do the work. I also had been working hard to rebuild my practice of massage and energy work in Santa Barbara. I had the limiting thought that if I went to Greece I would mess up my practice that was building beautifully. I also still would have standing bills for rent, car, and utilities with no income while away. Complete panic set in. I arranged to see Marilyn, who had become a good friend, for some coaching. She asked me, "Do you have faith and trust in Spirit?" I replied with a yes. She had me physically lean on her and then she stepped away. I didn't fall since I hadn't really trusted and didn't surrender completely. She suggested that was how I trusted Spirit. She had me lean again and I really counted on her to catch me this time.

She wondered if I had any experiences where I trusted God and things worked out. Marilyn said any past experiences were proof I could trust and things would work out; they were times I had slain the dragon of fear. I shared that when Frank first became ill he was very concerned about money since neither one of us could work as he needed 24-hour care. I told him I would handle all the money issues and for him to focus on getting well. I went into the living room and told God

I was turning this over to Him since I couldn't deal with it and Frank's illness. Within two hours I first got a phone call from my first boyfriend who was still a friend. I didn't mention our money issues, but told him of Frank's diagnosis. He asked for my bank details because he was wiring me $5,000. Secondly, an hour later the doorbell rang and it was a special delivery from dear friends with a check for $5,000 to help us and again I didn't tell them of our financial need.

After Frank died I had another testament that I could trust. I had credit card debts of $37,000 when I became a widow. I calculated it would take several lifetimes to just pay the interest alone. This was a very heavy burden. I was told I must fill out reams of paperwork for Frank's workplace upon his death, but I wouldn't get any money as he hadn't worked there long enough. Well, I did receive two checks from them that paid the debt off by one hundred dollars! I called his boss and he said to cash the checks.

Notice when we have fears our thoughts go to the worst case scenario. It is good to realize you don't have to believe everything you think even when it is a tenacious thought. With this coaching I decided I would go to Greece for a short period to handle things. Marilyn asked why I was limiting Spirit by thinking I could go only for a brief time. She said you either really trust or you don't. She reminded me that there is no time in Spirit and how could a couple of more weeks make much difference. Of course, at the same time my father in his most critical parent tone questioned, "What are you doing to your practice by going to Greece?" My insightful sister admonished me to listen to my heart and not Dad. I listened to my heart and held firmly to my proof where I had wisely trusted in the past. I went for five weeks. It turned out I needed that much time to accomplish all the tasks, my practice didn't suffer in the least, and all bills were paid on time. By facing my fear straight on and taking action I empowered myself. I saw the rabbit in the situation and I wanted to hug that rabbit. I wrote this in my journal:

> *I have been here in Greece nearly a month, it is going by so rapidly. I feel so strong, confident and powerful! It has been so good for my soul and I am filling my cup. It has been so empowering. My leap of faith to come was a wise decision and I was here on the first anniversary of Frank's graduation into spirit. Once I dared to risk in spite of my fear I was empowered.*

Fear often paralyzes, but action will break its grip. Don't let fear make your decisions. I had a dream while struggling with my fear around money. In the dream a powerful healing woman chooses me as a subject for a demonstration. She wants me to travel to another country and I say that maybe I'll go if I can find a less expensive way to travel. She told me emphatically to change that kind of thinking; it has to go! So my inner knowing was telling me to let go of such a limiting fear.

To work toward a positive expectation of money I played with the word abundance in my journal. I sketched a bunny dancing. I was determined to change from a limiting fear to a loving energy of supply.

Loneliness

I experienced deep loneliness during the grieving process. At times I felt forsaken and I yearned to have Frank back. When I needed holding the most, he wasn't there to embrace me and comfort me. I not only lost my husband but also my best friend. The hole in my life was huge as I'm sure it is in yours. I know you can relate to these feelings. I wrote in my journal:

> *I am feeling abandoned today. I know Frank didn't intentionally leave me, but I still feel like an orphan. Now I must not abandon myself! Marilyn says when we suppress our emotions we are abandoning ourselves. "Be there for yourself, live your sphere of possibilities," she encouraged.*

The concept of abandonment showed up in my dreams as well. One night I dreamed that I was with Frank and he said, "I know you want to be with me, but I don't want to be with you." I woke up very upset. Another dream I was with him and he acted strange, as if he was interested in another woman. I was sobbing and really miserable when I woke up. Later I went to the drug store and I was drawn to look at the rack of greetings cards, and one in particular caught my eye. This is what it said: "Our love is a promise, a promise forever!" I knew it was Frank pointing it out to me. I bought the card. My dreams confirmed that I was feeling abandoned.

At one of my energy sessions with Peter I told him of the unbearable longing and the haunting loneliness I lived with every day. He worked a lot on grounding my energy and told me to stay with my longing and aloneness. He explained that they would fuel me to express this longing with my heart and voice which would draw what I needed to keep moving forward. He cautioned to not push the feelings away, but to embrace them. They needed holding as I did.

I wrote in my journal:

> *Lately I get this yearning type of feeling when I think of Frank. It feels like there are hands reaching, stretching out of my heart center. I feel it physically and emotionally. Longing!! It's been so much time since I've even been held or tenderly cuddled. It is almost a year since we made love. I miss the cuddling most, today anyway.*

You will see that you can feel alone even in a large crowd. You often feel desolate and lonely for the one person that you can't be with now. You yearn for that one person in your barren lifescape. I would catch myself searching for Frank everywhere I went. Edna St. Vincent Millay aptly expressed it when she wrote "Where you used to be, there is a hole in the world, which I find myself constantly walking around in the daytime, and falling in at night. I miss you like hell."

I felt so solitary as I adjusted to Frank's death. I knew I wasn't alone spiritually. I had a beautiful experience just a few days before Frank's illness surfaced that reinforced this belief. I was receiving a massage and energy session. I was very deeply relaxed and suddenly I had a vision. I was with Christ and He held my face in His hands and looked intently into my eyes. He said, "I am ALWAYS with you." He repeated the words with even more emphasis. "KNOW I AM ALWAYS WITH YOU!" Happy tears flooded my face and I got chills of truth or what I call my God bumps. It was a deeply profound experience. I recalled it often during my grief journey and felt an inner comfort rise up inside me. Spirit is always there for you as well, whether you have a vision or not. **Even if you are on your own you are not alone.**

A dear friend of mine who was a chaplain for Hospice of Santa Barbara, Timothy Larson, explained this beautifully in this excerpt from his poem:

The Grace of Illness
The desert of lonely isolation is
being transformed
Into a lush garden of solitude.....
What began as debilitating despair
Has become vigorous hope....
The tightening bands of anxious distress
Have opened my heart
to the dance of grace....

I recall wondering if there would be a greater sense of loneliness once my grief work wasn't so intense and time consuming. I did find that to be true for a while, but finally, like a disappearing morning mist, it gradually dissipated.

Try to use this time as an opportunity to get to know you on a deeper level. While it can be intense, it is also a chance for self-discovery. You will draw on untouched resources and explore new dimensions of your being; it can stretch your limits. Yes, the process is wrought with growing pains and a prevalent sense of rawness. As you break open and your normal definitions of who you are dissolve, a new and glorious being can emerge with time. You are in a period of transformation. I felt at times that I was merging with the vastness of my spirit as the shell of my prior self cracked and opened. I often needed solitude while I was morphing.

I did find it was an irony that I felt so lonely and yet I wanted solitude. I needed to hibernate, especially in the early stages of my process, as I described. In winter, nature withdraws. I was definitely going through a wintertime in my life and instinctively took shelter within. We often need to be on our own to delve into the depth of our being as we wait for spring to appear. It is somewhat like what a seed experiences when first sprouting underground.

I wrote this poem, in my journal:

Spring
I embrace the grief:
Explore the heaviness of my spirit
Experiencing it fully, deeply
I feel the transformation begin.
As I merge with the vastness of my soul
I remember my wholeness and prepare for spring.

Anger

Anger is a powerful emotion that also plays havoc in the life of a griever. It was a good thing that earlier in my life, I had made peace with the feeling. I accepted it as an emotional color on my palette of possibilities. During Frank's illness and after his death, anger would tear though me with the fury of a hurricane. I was always one to avoid conflict and didn't like to see displays of anger, even from someone else. A fighting tigress was born at this crossroads in my life. It began with the need to battle for so many things with the medical world. Frank was too ill to fight for himself so I pounced to the forefront. I even got enraged for those who had no advocate to speak for them.

I also got mad at God. I don't believe that God dishes out illness, but I didn't understand how it is decided who gets a miracle. I was angry at Frank for dying, for leaving me alone, and leaving all the important papers scattered. I was angry that it took me nine months to find his will. I was upset we didn't get life insurance immediately with his new job. We opted to wait until January, but in the meantime he got ill Christmas morning. I could continue with a list of things I was angry at, but you get the idea and I am sure you can make a list of grievances just as long. I can only imagine the rage you could be dealing with right now if your loved one lost their life due to someone's negligence or because of purposeful violence. Again, if any emotion is too big for you to handle on your own, please reach for professional assistance.

Sometimes you might want to throw something, especially if you are feeling rage or even a milder version of anger. In my support groups we brainstormed ideas to move and release such strong feelings. Here are some of the ideas we came up with: throw breakable items into a recycle bin; hit a tennis ball against a wall; chop wood; punch a punching bag; play racquet ball or tennis; hit on a pillow or go to a batting cage. At a fair, I found the perfect outlet in a game. I smashed the mechanical gophers with a mallet as they came out of various holes. I even won a prize! I should add here that I would never do that to real live gophers. It helps to make sound as you do these things. All of these activities get the emotion and energy moving and they give you something to do. You are taking action in a constructive manner, and taking control of the emotion rather than allowing it to control you.

I worked anger out through meditation, writing, exercise, massage, and energy work. A year after Frank became ill I had a great massage. I had a major release. I wrote in my journal:

I finally got in touch with my anger concerning Frank's death. I felt like a lioness trying to protect her cub and I couldn't save him. The anguish, the anger, the rage poured out of me. I lashed out; my hand even became a claw. I snarled and growled and even screamed. Then I sobbed and sobbed. The tears are here again as I write and my hand is shaking. I even felt anger with God. I had to say out loud: "Why? Why God? Why Frank? How do you decide who gets the miracles?" I didn't expect answers, but the frozen words had to be expressed aloud. I cried and cried, nose running and coughing. The masseuse was working deeply above and just below my breasts. What pain physically, but it was the bridge to release the harbored anger. I had held it long enough. I am so glad I am able to get massages and energy work. Thank goodness for bartering.

I also think it is wise to choose your battles, especially when your energy is depleted by grief. On Frank's birthday I received a nasty letter from the landlord we had while in Santa Cruz. She said she wasn't returning any of the $500 deposit. I was so angry as I had even pulled weeds out of the front garden beds by flashlight before I moved out. Money was incredibly tight for me at that time so I did everything to guarantee I would get the deposit back. My first reaction was to fight her decision which would mean taking her to small claims court, a five-hour drive away. After cooling down, I thought it was best not to give her any of my precious energy. I was in such a weakened state after Frank's death and I just didn't have the stamina to deal with this. She knew that too. If I had been in a stronger space I would have contested. I did write her a letter and explained how I felt and hoped she would be more compassionate with her future tenants and others who crossed her path. I did hear later that someone else turned her in for illegal actions with her rental properties and she received huge fines. That was quick karma.

I had an energy session with Peter and told him I had been feeling some rare pain in my hands and they were stiff. He said he detected blocked energy that was trying to release out of my hands. Energy normally releases from your hands and fingers as well as from your feet and toes as the meridians of energy begin and end in these areas. I felt anger as he worked to release the energy. I realized that I had been feeling angry since my hands began to bother me. He suggested I hit on pillows and think of what I was angry or frustrated about. I knew it was about not finding Frank's will, not having Frank, anger with Dad, and anger with Frank that he didn't leave papers more organized. Peter told me to get my blood moving: to swim, walk up hills, bike etc. Such activity would help to move my anger. He recommended that I eat dandelion greens or bitter greens that would help my liver. He explained that in Chinese medicine, anger, especially repressed anger, injures the liver. Using acupuncture he worked on my liver and gall bladder points.

I drew a sketch of a clenched fist to be painted red in front of a healthy hand in warm colors with energy radiating out the fingers. Flames of fire are behind the clenched fist.

Another day when anger was seething in me, I wrote down everything that was making me mad and folded the paper and burned it in a safe way. Do something, take action; it helps as it transforms the energy of the emotion.

Please acknowledge any anger you feel and attend to the emotion. You don't want it to take root and become bitterness. Remember: it takes more energy to repress an emotion than to process it.

Depression

Depression is a normal reaction in grief. I told you I wasn't allowed to even say the word depressed growing up so this was a new emotion for me to process. When I couldn't leave my apartment and sat and rocked myself without a rocking chair, I didn't know what was going on. My sister, a counselor, told me I was the "D" word and then said depressed. I was shocked. Me? Depressed? She quickly added that of course, I was, and she would have been worried if I wasn't. She gave me permission to be just what I was and I give you the same. There are things to observe to see if you are depressed. Is there a change in your appetite? Are you sleeping more or less than normal? Has your concentration diminished? Do you have poor memory? Are you fatigued, more irritable? Are you able to handle your daily responsibilities, or are you completely withdrawing from people and activities?

If you see these signs in your experience and behavior, they are normal. Take notice, however, if they continue too long, if they are overwhelming, or you are totally unable to handle your responsibilities. Don't self-medicate with drugs or alcohol, but rather seek professional help.

I would like to conclude this section on emotions with a different way to frame the sense of breaking down. When you feel broken down, try looking at is as breaking open. This leaves room for hope of growth. Your broken open heart can expand and learn to hold even greater love and compassion.

Heartfelt Suggestions ⟡

Now it is time to go to a quiet place where you can take some time for yourself. Bring a notebook and pen. Place your hand over your heart and close your eyes. Take several slow deep breaths down into your lower belly. Allow your breath to guide you to the peaceful place within your heart. Now open your eyes and begin reading and reflect on the suggestions. Remember this is part of your conscious mourning and it is sacred work.

1. Are there specific thoughts about something that you can re-frame to improve your emotional experience of it?

2. Are you attempting to block any feelings or are you allowing your emotions to flow?

3. How are you constructively expressing your feelings?

4. Can you choose more life-enhancing ways to give voice to your emotions?

5. Have you tried journaling, nature, meditation, group support, professional guidance or other ways to cope?

6. Are you abandoning you?

CHAPTER FIVE

RECALIBRATING: Mind and Body

Thoughts

YOUR THOUGHTS CAN EITHER be comforting and supportive, or torturing and unmerciful. In Anita Shreve's novel *The Pilot's Wife*, this experience is aptly described as a widow being frequently drenched and assailed by memories, and buffeted and chilled by thoughts. I recall some twenty-five years ago reading that you can choose what you think. At first I thought that was impossible; thoughts just came into my head, right? I think today that has been one of the most valuable things I have learned in my life. Knowing this is possible helped me immensely in my grieving process. If I don't like the feelings that come with a thought, I can consciously change my thinking process to a concept that I choose.

This was greatly tested during my mourning. Grief triggered such painful and horrific thinking. Before Frank died the fearful thoughts of losing him haunted me. After he died I relived all the trauma of his illness and death over and over creating mental whiplash. It was as if a persistent loop of agony played relentlessly in my mind. At times it felt like a negative magnet was pulling the offending thoughts to the forefront of my thinking. To combat this, when I caught myself in a downward spiral, I would pick a good memory to concentrate on instead of dwelling on the negative one. Often my thinking was like a radio station that drifts to another nearby station, as my thinking would bleed back to the upsetting words and images. Sometimes I had to wrestle to bring my attention to healthier thinking, as some excruciatingly painful negative thoughts seemed to run on autopilot.

As you can imagine, your mind can create roadblocks on your mourning journey. But as your thoughts go round and round, recreating the same gruesome feelings, you can find an exit and take another road. Work to allow your inner observer to become aware of what your thoughts are creating. Then allow that Inner Wise One within your heart to direct your thinking to a more beneficial pattern. Your thoughts are very powerful. Where your attention goes, energy flows. Negative thought patterns can make you feel worse. Your thoughts can rip open the scar tissue creating ever fresh wounds from your loss. Be very patient with yourself, but keep up your determination to choose more beneficial thoughts.

Start to observe your thoughts and how they make you feel. Really look at what you are thinking. I wrote them in my journal. I witnessed such thoughts as: *I can't stand this! This just can't be true! How am I going to live through this? Can I take care of myself? Why Frank?* Some days it was very difficult to stop the words.

In one of our classes, Marilyn had a person stand and put their dominant arm out in front of them. She asked them to resist with their arm as she pushed down near their elbow. They held strong.

Then she asked them to think of a negative thought as she pushed downward and their arm was weaker and noticeably went down. When the person was asked to think of a positive thought, once again they were very strong. I went to Marilyn after class and asked her to do it with me so I could feel the difference in my body. It was quite astonishing how my negative thinking affected my strength. I suggest you try this with someone in order to know viscerally the power of your thoughts. This process is called muscle testing and never fails to point out the truth of your thoughts.

It is very important to monitor your self-talk. Are you encouraging or discouraging yourself? I can catch myself thinking things I would hate to hear from another person. Be a kind and supportive friend to yourself. Do not recycle the sludge in your life. Reliving it over and over in your mind is often more damaging than the original negative! I noted in my journal that I was working on this with the negative memories concerning Frank's illness and death, but it was easier said than done. As I would become aware of disturbing feelings, I would turn my attention to witness what I was thinking at the moment. This undoubtedly uncovered a discouraging and upsetting thought.

When you begin to watch your emotions and thought connections you will catch when you cross over the road divider and are off track. It will alert you to get back on the path you want to travel toward peace and balance. Often it is your thoughts that keep fueling miserable feelings. I found it helpful to have a specific good memory to switch to easily when needed. To refocus the ideas flowing through my head I made a list of funny experiences I had shared with Frank. Just reading that list at least made me smile and often I laughed out loud.

Beliefs

A limiting thought can be as detrimental as a negative one. Thinking a limiting thought is like driving a car with the emergency brake on, or living life with a straitjacket restricting you. One you have put on yourself, I might add. Your beliefs can be blinders to other possibilities, leaving you unable to even think out of the box. Work to overcome the self-imposed boundaries set by any limiting thought or belief. For instance, clinging to the role of victim can inhibit your progress through mourning.

I try to reframe how I look at something to improve how I feel about it. I am reminded of a time before Frank became ill. We had just moved to the area of Santa Cruz, CA. There is a treacherous highway leading to Santa Cruz that I swore I never would drive. Well, I learned to never say never. I had to drive Frank for his radiation and chemo treatments for ten weeks, five days a week, back and forth on that highway. It took an hour and a half each way. I knew I needed to reframe my thinking about this stretch of road in order to make the trips bearable. I had to befriend this highway. I chose to look at it as a bridge to his wellness. The time on these journeys would be precious time with just the two of us without any medical interventions. I played relaxation tapes and special music. This time became sacred for both of us. What thoughts can you reframe to make your journey more palatable? Transformation or metamorphosis can be difficult enough without adding unhelpful or detrimental thinking to the equation. Be open to see things from a different perspective.

You have free will; you can observe your beliefs and rewrite the scripts that you live by. After Frank died I made a list of beliefs I wanted to change. I was told from an early age that I had no musical ability, that I was tone deaf. I tackled that erroneous belief by starting harp lessons four months after Frank died. I explained to Barbara, my teacher, that the biggest obstacle was the limiting belief I had around doing anything musical. It wasn't too long before I had my first recital playing *The Little Harpist* alongside of a group of children.

Another belief I wanted to change was a negative body image. Our society doesn't help women with this self-concept. I decided to face this one head on, or more aptly, body on. I volunteered to model nude at an art school. I figured if I was ever going to be motivated to have an out of body experience, it would be modeling with a group of students in a circle around me. I did go into a meditative state and had a very interesting realization. At one point I couldn't label what I was feeling. Then it dawned on me that I was feeling elegant, the absolute last possibility I could image. I still have far from a perfect body, but I am comfortable in my skin now. Both of these examples definitely took me way out of my comfort zone, but grief had shattered my comfort zone anyway. I encourage you to make a list of your limiting beliefs or attitudes that you want to change. You are in a period of transformation anyway – go for it.

I had a dream when I was reviewing my beliefs and attitudes. I was hauling big boxes of trash out of the house. I pulled out old blankets to wash and keep and tossed others. Some were ones my family had had when I was a child. I wrote after the dream in my journal that I thought it referred to the purification in my life at the time. I was looking at my old patterns and beliefs, cleaning up some and throwing others out.

Worry

"Worry never robs tomorrow of its sorrow, but only saps today of its strength." ~ A. J. Cronen.

Worry is a pattern that we had best discard. Most grievers I have shared with tended to worry quite a bit. My mother taught me that worrying is like paying interest on a loan you haven't even taken from the bank. Look back at your life. Most of the things which you worried about never happened. When such a thought attacked my peace, I would say to myself, *Thank you for sharing. I'm a capable person who can take care of my life.* As I took on so many new responsibilities after Frank died I would often worry if I could handle it all. I would barrage myself in inner negative chatter. I would stop once I caught myself and think, *I can handle… !* I was determined to control my thoughts rather than have them controlling me. We can either be pitiful or powerful.

So many people do what I call "awfulizing"; looking for the worst case scenario and espousing it. Negative thinking is misuse of your imagination to create things you don't want. Such toxic mind scripts are not life enhancing. Choose thoughts consciously that will turn your steering wheel of life in the best direction. Are you on the road you want to take? Choose what you want to concentrate on. If the negatives cause you pain, change your thinking. Your attitude is often more important than the facts of the situation.

It is better to affirm *I am courageous. I am a survivor,* rather than *I can't do anything right. I'll never recover from this. My life is ruined forever and this pain will never end.* I put some positive affirmations I wrote for myself in my car, on the refrigerator, and on the bathroom mirror. Just seeing these reminded me to choose life enhancing words in my outer and inner dialogues. See what works for you.

To rebuild my self-esteem, I wrote down some of my recent accomplishments that I felt were significant. I realized later that almost all I had listed were internal things like becoming my own best friend, learning to be without doing, honoring all my feelings, and becoming non-resistant. I didn't list degrees or jobs. As I was raised to be an overachiever, I was proud of myself for this list of feelings rather than "things."

Check what you say to yourself. Are your thoughts in your best interest? Will your thoughts and actions increase your energy and assist you on your *Resilient Heart*® Journey, or decrease your abilities to deal with your life situation and keep you stuck in pain and misery? You can change your mind. You are responsible for managing your thoughts and feelings. I often would affirm that I was flowing into better choices.

Why?

There is a common thread of painful thinking that grievers torture themselves with namely *Why….? Why did my loved one die? Why didn't I do… ? What if… ?* This kind of thinking is fruitless and painful. There is often no answer and this is a sure way to drive yourself crazy. I suggest when you go down this route to tell yourself, *Today I'm going to let go of my need to know and just go with the flow.* Quit trying to understand and just experience for now. Some things will never be understood and need to be accepted without resistance. Until we change our thoughts, nothing changes. Look back at this period of time in your life with grace. You did the best you could with the information you had and in the circumstances you were in. You can't go back, so try not to judge yourself and be gentle with yourself as your loved one would be. It is better to ask, *Now that this has happened, what do I do?* Sometimes that is forgiving yourself or someone else. A friend of mine was driving the car that crashed and killed her best friend. She was able to forgive herself and decided to help other grievers which she did for many years.

Bring yourself to the present rather than buffeting yourself with the past. Here's a reminder: **a quick way to bring yourself to the present is to observe your breath.** Let your heart and your breath become your touchstone to becoming present. Put your hand over your heart and close your eyes. Breathe peace into your heart and think of coming back to yourself, to center. Exhale any tortuous and turbulent thoughts that are currently engulfing you. Let your heart and breath be a solid rock for you to grab on to during your mental and emotional storms; your port in the storm, if you will. Visualize an upright center of a child's spinning top centered and balanced as you slowly breathe in and out. Each breath brings you more peace, serenity, and more stability.

Body

Not only are your emotions and thoughts affected by grief, but so is your body. You might experience sleep disruptions, fatigue, headaches, loss of appetite, heart palpitations, knotted muscles, difficulty swallowing, dizziness, or the inability to follow your normal exercise regime. Often I would catch myself holding my breath or breathing shallowly and rapidly. It is very important that you take care of your body while on your mourning voyage. Marilyn told us to think of supporting our body like the four legs of a table help keep it balanced. Each of the four legs represented water intake, proper diet, exercise, or sleep/rest. We were to look back to our prior week and see which was our weakest leg or support. The weakest was to be our primary focus the following week. At the beginning of my journey, I didn't do very well in any of these categories. I didn't feel like cooking for one, as it was a constant reminder I was on my own. I realized finally that I was eating mainly canned food. I had always told my family for years that eating canned food was like eating dead food. Now I was eating what I considered dead food! What was that telling my body? Exactly! I weaned myself off of that eating regime. I began making large dishes of something like eggplant parmesan and freezing portions. Buying a large bag of fresh salad kept meals simple. There were delicious and nutritional soups in cartons that I could easily heat up. Ultimately, I set the table beautifully by putting pretty placemats, matching napkins, and fresh flowers on it. Try to eat healthy while you are grieving as mourning takes a lot of energy.

My sleep patterns were very erratic to say the least. Normally I slumber peacefully all through the night. I don't usually have nightmares, but they persisted for some time after Frank died. Why does everything seem so much worse in the middle of the night? I would wake in the dark and unpack my suitcases of worries, fears, and challenges. It was at this time that I stopped drinking caffeine after five in the afternoon to encourage restful sleep. Make sure you are exercising as that will aid in better sleep, but not just before you go to bed. If you don't sleep well at night, try to find times in your day to rest and perhaps nap. A warm bath before bed induces relaxation. When I had a particularly rough time to fall or stay asleep, I used special CDs of music that balanced the two hemispheres of the brain. I had to wear a headset so that they would be effective, but they really helped me.

I had a difficult time getting any exercise at first; I couldn't make myself leave my apartment to even take a walk. I began scheduling appointments for walks. It especially helped to arrange to meet a friend for a hike. I committed to doing exercises with a TV program daily. About a year after Frank died I decided to join a gym and really dedicate myself to an exercise program. I figured I could take control of this area of my life when in so many areas I felt out of control. Look in your life for areas you can control and make some movement toward taking control. Remember that exercise helps you release pent up emotional energy and helps you to relax. It is best if you can get outside and be in nature, but at least walk around your home. Movement helps you release your emotions, aids in softening tight muscles, and assists you in experiencing sound sleep.

Your body also needs water to function properly. I would fill a large pitcher with water in the morning, put it in the refrigerator, and my goal was to drink it that day. That way I realized how much I consumed. In a nutritional course I attended, I learned that nothing is a substitute for water. Coffee, tea etc., are all digested as food. The body's main organs have priority access to the water you drink for your survival. Most people are dehydrated and that is without the added stress of grief draining their system.

Unfortunately, widows and widowers often become ill after their spouse dies. I did some research and found this quote in an article by the Harvard Medical School. "Recently widowed women show reduced activity of natural killer cells (cells that attack viruses and tumors) and higher levels of the stress hormone cortisol compared with women whose husbands are still alive. Persistently elevated levels of stress hormones can reduce immunity, raise blood pressure and cholesterol, and induce heart rhythms."

When you lose a loved one you are experiencing a major trauma. The only time I have had a migraine headache was after a very stressful situation. The doctor explained that it was my body having a tough time readjusting when the stress was gone. My doctor explained that we adapt to stress, but then often the ability to return to the state before the trauma can be difficult to achieve and symptoms can occur, like migraine headaches. When you are traumatized, often you want to be out of your body, away from the deep pain. I know I did. However, you can't function very well when you are beside yourself. Bring your consciousness to your feelings around the trauma. Where do you feel something in your body? What does it feel like? Stay with the sensation, breathe into it, and it will shift. Bringing your awareness to your emotions and your body can move you toward balance if you allow rather than resist the sensation.

Bodywork

I found bodywork to be a very important tool in my mourning. Being a bodyworker myself, I know the benefits in general for massage and energy work. I know you can hold emotional trauma in your "soma" or body. I had endured the most devastating experience of my life, dealing with Frank's illness and subsequent death. I knew I didn't have the time to take care of the effects to my body while he was coping with cancer, but I was determined to find help after he died. I had held tight so long taking care of everything and trying to keep the fear of losing him at bay, but I knew I was depleted and bound with pent-up emotions. You often don't realize how much you are holding in and how tense you are until you relax even a bit. For me, the place I can let go and relax the most is on a massage table. I received regular bodywork from friends who are fellow therapists and gave them IOUs for when I could give back. I also got regular energy sessions from Peter Hurley who is an acupuncturist and uses several modalities of other energy work in his practice.

I knew Reiki energy sessions would help me and I made sure I got them. I am a Reiki Master/Teacher and I have been trained in other energy modalities as well, so I had a large pool of my students to call upon for my needs. The most important thing is to go to someone you feel comfortable with. I also picked people who could work with my emotional releases which were my intention and I certainly experienced this release with them. The more you can let go and surrender while on the massage table, the greater your body can relax on a deeper and deeper level. At that place of surrender, your body's innate wisdom can guide you to a more peaceful state and your blocked emotions can move out of your body. Often you don't even need to know exactly what is being released. I think this is a great quality about bodywork; you don't need to talk and talk about your issues. **Your body and being want to be in a place of balance and if you get out of the way, they will go back to equilibrium.** It is an excellent opportunity to practice surrendering and letting go of resistance while receiving a massage. If you feel any discomfort physically or emotionally, think of relaxing into it and concentrate on your breathing. This will bring you to the present, the place of power.

I have had several counseling therapists call on me to do body and energy work on their clients since they are not permitted to touch an individual. These counselors realized how the body can store issues that aren't resolved. They wanted their people to benefit from traditional counseling combined with physical work.

An added gift of massage is that you often crave non-sexual touch while grieving. It is a great way to feel pampered. I suggest you set an intention for any work you get and share it with your practitioner. My intentions usually were about releasing some emotion like anger, fear, or the trauma of Frank's illness. Other times I needed balance, clarity, or peaceful relaxation.

In both massage and energy sessions, I felt my throat clearing. I sometimes coughed during the work. Peter encouraged me saying my rawness was beautiful, and being vulnerable and staying with my emotions was a good thing. It was very difficult to do at times; I lost so many defenses through the rawness and felt so exposed. I found as I cleared my throat area I was more conscious of my pained heart. At the conclusion of one particular session with Peter, he said I was an expression of an exposed heart, willing to feel. I often felt a great heaviness in my chest area. Peter and other practitioners gave me valuable feedback on how I was doing on my journey. I was told that I was going forward to meet my pain and wasn't resisting it. By doing this it eventually led to more peace and clarity. It helped to receive their feedback when I found it difficult see myself objectively.

I learned in my training for Polarity Therapy, an energy-based system including bodywork, that grief is connected with the element of ether and that the energy center in your throat is often stirred by grief. Self-expression is key to open the throat: music, sounds, meditation, and expressing your emotions were recommended in Polarity Therapy. I did feel so much constriction in my throat and heart area while I grieved. When working with ether you must ground often. Getting out in nature is wise. Also breathing up balancing energy from the earth into your feet and body is a good way to ground. Working on your big toes is good and helps release your grief. Jokingly, I shared in a grief support group that we should perhaps suck our thumbs which is a lot easier than your big toes. We had a good laugh which we all needed. It was noted that my advice was the most unusual they had received. Ether gets you in touch with your true nature. It strips you down to what is your essence. The energies that are directed by the lower centers of your being, such as survival, sex, and power are subordinate to the grief. Grieving can make you very receptive to Spirit. When you grieve you experience a force beyond the ego. I often felt after any type of bodywork that I was coming home to myself, reclaiming the true essence of who I am. I highly recommend that you have some bodywork while you are on your mourning sojourn.

Sound Healing

There are many ways to give voice to your emotions and thoughts. I worked with everything I could find. I studied the power of sound in healing for at least twelve years before Frank died. Our ancient relatives used sound through chanting and drum rhythms to create balance. Today modern medicine is using ultrasound. I used sound for my healing in several ways. I listened to particular music that I resonated with, I learned to play the harp, and I used my voice to express my emotions. Sound can be a powerful way to release.

I treated myself to a subscription to the local symphony's classical season. I would sit and totally relax my body concentrating on each area before the performance. As I listened I held the intention to allow the music to flow through my entire being, body, mind, and spirit. I could feel the vibrations of sound relaxing me even deeper. I also listened to relaxing music at home, but normally live music worked better. The music that balances the right and left hemispheres of the brain also entrained me to peace. I also listened over and over again to a CD given to us when Frank was ill. *Hope* is the title and it was a compilation of songs and singers produced by the Mormon Church.

Learning to play the harp also allowed the vibrations to penetrate my body and was a transformational experience. Luckily you can't make a harp sound bad even when you are learning. It vibrated in my heart and throat where I felt my grief the most. When I carried the harp to a grief group, I encouraged others to strum it and feel the healing vibrations in their bodies. I wanted them to allow the frequencies to heal their hearts.

Jonathan Goldman, a writer, musician, teacher, and an authority on sound healing, described toning:

> *"Toning is a generic term to describe the use of the voice for release of pain and stress, and to help align imbalanced portions of the body. Sighing, moaning, groaning, and other sounds we frequently make are all aspects of toning, as are the sounding of different vowels." (www.HealingSounds.com)*

In the early 90s I took a wonderful voice workshop with Jill Purce. Jill teaches voice for psychological, emotional, spiritual, and physical healing, meditation, relaxation, and the reduction of stress. I learned to harness the healing and transformative power of sound using Mongolian and Tibetan overtone chanting. Just listening to these chants is amazing, but having the sounds originate from within is even more powerful. She adheres to the principle that sound is both healing and transformational. You can rid yourself of the pain and hurt of traumas. Jill claims, "If you liberate the voice, you liberate the human body." (www. HealingVoice.com)

Knowing how powerful using your voice can be for healing, I found Christa Ray, a local sound instructor, when I returned to Santa Barbara. Again I needed someone to take me by the hand and lead me while I was mourning. A small group of us met weekly for her sounding course. She feels that the voice is an intermediary between the head and the heart, your thoughts and feelings. Sometimes she had us tune within and give sound to what we were feeling, just a sound not words. She encouraged us to honor not dismiss any negative states. So I put sound to my grief. She said that by sounding the feeling, a big grounded space opens to you. We practiced using vowel sounds. We usually worked in pairs which made it easier to open up and make sound as there wasn't an audience bigger than one. I was surprised how it worked to move the emotion by giving it a chance to express. No one even needed to know what feeling you were sounding. After you sounded anything you were currently experiencing in your life, your partner was to mirror your existing emotional sound and then to move for a sound to represent your wholeness. This gives you options and your pain is witnessed, acknowledged, and often shifted toward wholeness and balance. For instance, if you feel fear, become the fear and sound it, but stay open to love. Sounding the fear can help it move toward love. She described pain as constricted love. The course was quite powerful. This type of work with sound can align you to a template of wholeness. The voice is the muscle of the soul. I know singing feeds my sister's soul. It is one of the main ways she relaxes. I was more comfortable just making sounds rather than singing in front of others. You could try putting a vowel sound to your grief while driving or in the shower if you prefer to try it alone.

Another way I used sound was by speaking up for myself. I voiced my needs even if that meant changing plans. I told people like my father that he couldn't communicate with me in the manner he was used to using. I stood up for my need not to return to work immediately after Frank died. When I was ready to work I championed my decision to listen to my heart and stick with my massage/energy practice rather than returning to consultant work. You know what is best for you; speak your needs and beliefs.

Dancing

I found dancing a wonderful way to release and move my body. My dear mother said it was her dancing in her dad's farmhouse that saved her when he died and also when her brother died the year before. She was only nineteen when she had lost all of her immediate family. Her mom died when she was only four and her brother's plane was shot down in WWII. I have always loved dancing, so I decided to try dancing on my own in my apartment. Then I learned of a dance that was held weekly at a local Unitarian Church called Dance Away where everyone was doing their own thing. There were all styles of dance and people danced alone and some as couples. It was perfect. First I decided to dance my grief. Later as I danced I recalled beautiful memories of dancing throughout my life: on a beach in Greece; around a May pole; with drill teams; and special dances with Frank. There were so many good dancing memories. My feet were sore at the end of the night; it was a great evening. I went several times.

Later in my journal I penned:

> Life can be a dance flowing with the given notes or musical phrases. I can dance harmoniously when I don't resist the music that is given me. Resistance seems to be a big issue right now for me. I must learn to accept what is. I looked up the word resistance in the word origin book. It comes from a tank or pool which is standing and stagnant as opposed to running water. If I don't allow my emotions to flow through me like water or a dance, they become stagnant and I experience resistance. I will try to let my emotions flow like a river. I will try to dance with them.

I saw a reference to a program that danced children's grief by expressing their emotional anguish through movement. In particular they danced anger, anxiety, and confusion. This was produced by the Bodiography Contemporary Ballet and was directed by Maria Caruso in Pittsburgh, Pennsylvania.

A few times in the sounding course I took, Christa had us add movement as we sounded our emotions. I liked the combination of vocals and body movements.

Movement creates flow. I encourage you to walk, dance, shake, shimmy, get bodywork and/or energy work to get unstuck and get your emotions and thoughts moving. You might want to try yoga, Tai Chi, or Qigong. How are you now moving through your life? Are you dancing, stumbling, skipping, standing, or sitting it out and just observing on the sidelines of life? Life is not a spectator sport. Sometimes little movements are huge… in the context of your life situation of grief. There are different rhythms for different times. Balance is not static.

So **releasing is about processing emotions through expression**. Clear limited thoughts and learn to choose life-enhancing words that uplift you. Nurture your body as you grieve by opting for healthy choices, all the while making peace with your loss and expressing your bereavement.

Heartfelt Suggestions

Now it is time to go to a quiet place where you can take some time for yourself. Bring a notebook and pen. Place your hand over your heart and close your eyes. Take several slow deep breaths down into your lower belly. Allow your breath to guide you to the peaceful place within your heart. Now open your eyes and begin reading and reflect on the suggestions. This is part of your conscious mourning and it is sacred work.

1. Are you witnessing your thoughts and feelings?

2. Are you taking control of your thinking and attempting to redirect negative or limiting thoughts to more uplifting choices?

3. Are you asking if your thoughts and worries are known truths or assumptions?

4. Have you become conscious how your thoughts orchestrate what you are feeling?

5. Are you checking weekly how you are eating, sleeping, exercising and drinking water?

6. Have you tried bodywork or energy work to assist you in your grief work?

7. Are you using music, sound or dance as a conscious tool?

CHAPTER SIX

RIPTIDES: Avoiding the Undertow

A RIPTIDE IS A STRETCH OF turbulent water in the sea caused by meetings of currents or abrupt changes in depth causing violent disturbance. On your *Resilient Heart*® Journey you will encounter many riptides. Some can be expected, like seasonal holidays, and some will completely catch you off guard like receiving a call and hearing a voice asking to speak to your loved one who has died. These currents usually have an undertow that pulls you below the surface of coping and won't easily let go.

These disturbances can come on quickly. I am reminded of the dry river beds in Africa that can quickly become raging waterways. The weather can be perfect one minute then suddenly a flash flood can send torrents of water washing down the river, carrying you into the deep currents of grief yet again. Carried by intense cutting emotions, the armor you have placed around yourself while grieving shatters.

I recommend you prepare for times that could trigger these emotional riptides, especially birthdays, anniversaries, and annual holidays. These are normally joyful occasions that you look forward to celebrating, but grief takes a huge toll and changes these landmarks in your year. What previously created anticipation often becomes sheer dread. Days meant for celebration are now filled with sorrow and anguish. I wanted to rip certain days out of the calendar. Every day after the death of a loved one is difficult, but on certain days your loss is even further highlighted. You can get through them and, in fact, grow through them by making wise decisions. **Making a plan for anticipated riptides gives you some control at a time when you often feel disempowered.**

As Thanksgiving, Christmas, and New Year's Eve approached, I knew I had to do them differently after Frank died. I was cautioned not to compare how I celebrated in the past with what I was going to do now in the present. I was very worried about the holidays as I have always loved the magic of the season. During grief, the celebrations underlined and punctuated with exclamation marks the tremendous hole in my life. I wasn't alone in my thoughts and feelings. Every single member of the grief group shared that they were having difficulties with the holiday season. The dread of this specific time was almost worse than the actuality of watching the joy and cheer of others.

Several books I read and what we recommended in hospice was to create new holiday traditions. At first, going to bed and pulling the covers over my head sounded like a better option, but I knew I had to make a plan. I could always change the plan as my needs warranted. Checking in and taking care of myself as I would for a special friend became my intention. Ideally you are a special friend to yourself. It was very important to keep courting myself during the holidays. I wanted to get through this time of the year, which seemed much longer this time round, with as much grace as possible. I also needed to give myself some kindness and not expect too much of myself. Holidays can be very stressful even when you aren't grieving, so be gentle and caring with yourself. Don't schedule or take on too much for where you are at emotionally. I knew I didn't want to put my grieving on a shelf so I made sure I had space to be alone.

When making holiday decisions, do what is best for you and your immediate family. A widow I met decided to take her children and go on a trip rather than do Christmas at home without her husband. She said that if she were doing Christmas at all, it had to be completely different. First I will share some pointers to help you get through the holidays, and then I will share some of the plans I and others created to cope with the riptides.

Tips for the Holidays

- You don't have to live up to your or anyone else's expectations. You are free to adapt to your ability.

- Creating a plan can help you navigate the riptides and give you some control.

- Do things in a different way; it will be unlike your usual celebration anyway due to your loss. I whittled down how I celebrated and made things more manageable. I didn't do all our normal traditions as they were just too painful to even consider. You might want to volunteer at a soup kitchen or reach out to others in another form of service.

- Nurture yourself, take care of your needs, and speak your desires. You might need a blend of time alone and time with others. I found it very difficult to be in crowds the first holiday season. I ordered gifts through catalogues that year and avoided malls.

- Allow all of your feelings to come forth even though this can be a much more highly emotional time. I can hear you asking, "Is that even possible?" Yes, it is. You might even experience a bit of pleasure seeping into your experiences. It is not disrespectful to your loved one if you find yourself smiling or laughing. You are allowed to enjoy yourself.

- Be true to yourself. Stay open to it all that comes up for you and embrace it all gently in your heart. I believe when you are connected to your *Resilient Heart*® and Inner Wise One you will feel some joy.

- Take time to honor your loved one rather than trying *not* to remember them which is impossible. What could you do as a tribute to them?

- Be open and ask for support if you need it. You might need a shoulder to cry on, a comforting hug, or someone to lend an open ear. There are online support groups that you can connect to twenty-four hours a day. By all means, ask for what you need to get through these extra difficult times.

Thanksgiving

My first Thanksgiving alone I had an invitation to join friends as my family all lived in another state. As I didn't want to be alone that day, when I got their invitation I was so thankful I cried. As a new tradition, I began writing thank you notes to the many wonderful people in my life who had been such an incredible support. I wrote Frank a letter telling him how thankful I was for the years he blessed my life. I included what I had gratitude for during his illness, like that he was his loving and gentle self even with brain tumors. It was good for me to focus on what was good during that time. One member of a grief support group said every Thanksgiving her family puts a paper on a table and all day individuals add what they are grateful for. They read the paper at the dinner table and then keep it in a special notebook with the blessings of past years.

Another family grieving the loss of a husband and father rented a small community center, held a mass, and decided to share their food by inviting a needy family to join them for their meal of thanksgiving.

A family that lost their son to cancer spent Thanksgiving Day taking meals to AIDS patients who were homebound. The mother said it kept them busy and made them feel better.

Christmas and Hanukkah

After Thanksgiving, I decided to whittle the rest of the holidays down to a more manageable size. I knew Christmas would be tough. Christmas morning was when Frank's first symptoms surfaced with the loss of his sight. I dreaded that anniversary as well as Christmas in general. I couldn't do things the way I always had. I sent very few cards. I didn't go buy a tree to decorate with our traditional ornaments but rather opted for a tiny grove of three small Norfolk pines in a pot that sat on a table. I liked that they were live trees. Decorating them quite simply with tiny white lights, crystal prisms, and one bedraggled snowflake from our first Christmas together seemed more appropriate. Hanging only my Christmas stocking was just too painful so I had to hang Frank's as well. These were the things that would grab me emotionally and clutch my heart and throat. I decided to write down wonderful Christmas memories with Frank and put them in his stocking.

I concentrated on the true meanings of the holidays. I studied the roots to many celebrations of different cultures for this special time. Rather than focusing on the outer expressions of the season I went for the inner approach. I didn't attend any Christmas parties that first year. It would take more time to reclaim the magic of the holiday. I found a card at a store; it was about the difficulty of the season when your heart and soul have experienced great loss. It mirrored my sentiments and I purchased it for myself.

I did go to see my family for several days around Christmas Day. It was good to be with them and have distractions of shopping and cooking together. I did feel an extreme heaviness in my heart, but I later realized that I was so concerned about messing up their holiday that I stifled some strong feelings of my own. This was very apparent when I received a massage after the holidays and found I was holding some repressed emotions and hadn't handled the holiday with as much grace as I figured.

I found Christmas Eve was the toughest. The last time Frank and I made physical love had been Christmas Eve. Certain carols triggered me and memories grabbed at my heart. I did take the memory candle I had made with pictures of Frank on the outside of the glass, and we lit it and the one we had made for my mother when she died several years before. Every Christmas since my mother died we get an angel from a tree with a child's age and needs. We buy gifts, as she always did, in her memory.

My sister's First United Methodist Church provides a Blue Christmas Service for those who are grieving the loss of a loved one. I have attended one of them and it was beautiful. I appreciated that they honored those in grief. The first Advent candle they lit was to remember those whom we had loved and lost. We paused to recall their name, their face, their voice, and the memory that binds them to us in this season. The second candle was lit to redeem the pain of loss: the loss of relationships, the loss of jobs, or the loss of health. We paused to gather up the pain of the past and offered it to God, asking that from God's hands we receive the gift of peace. The third candle was lit to remember ourselves this Christmas time. We paused and remembered these past weeks and months: the disbelief and anger, the down times, the poignancy of reminiscing, the hugs and handshakes of family and friends and all those who stood with us. We gave thanks for all the support we have known. The fourth candle was lit to remember our faith and the gift of hope which the Christmas story offers to us.

This church also makes prayer shawls for those needing comfort after a loss or in times of stress. Each shawl is filled with prayers from the person making it and the ministers of the church. When I received one I felt wrapped in love.

I also went to a Hanukkah party through the grief group. We had to open ten bottles of wine as each had turned to vinegar creating more grief. It did make us laugh which was healthy. We also shared some deep discussions. I was concerned how some of them make other grievers their whole life. Some had been on antidepressants for years since their spouse died. Others seem stuck in their grief and weren't trying to move forward. This wasn't what I wanted; I was determined to come out the other side of this ordeal.

My second holiday season after Frank's death was a bit better, but still very difficult. I wrote this in my journal:

> *It has been a rough couple of days. I decided to get a small, real Christmas tree this year. I love the magic of a tree and the lights. As I was driving to the corner where they were for sale I could feel emotions welling up. I thought, "You don't have to do this, Gail. You can turn around and go home."*

This was my first time to buy a tree alone. When picking our last tree together, we went to the same place we always did while living in Santa Barbara, California. All the beautiful memories of the past flooded through me as I drove to the tree lot. In New Jersey, we cut down our trees out in the country. Once, in Greece, we made a tree with pine limbs wired to a broom stick. In Bali, we used a palm frond and hung my earrings on it as ornaments. We loved Christmas and sharing it with friends and family. I wanted the wonder and mysteries of Christmas again so I drove on to the familiar tree lot to get my little tree.

One woman in my grief group avoided the whole holiday season. She didn't decorate and didn't participate in gift exchanges. She told her family ahead of time that she needed a complete change and she opted to go skydiving. Some people shared that other family members took on the job of decorating the tree. One man's children did all of it as he just couldn't face the task.

New Year's Eve

The next holiday hurdle was New Year's Eve. I made a plan to walk a labyrinth lit with white candles. As I walked into the spiral, I thought of letting go of my pain, and as I walked out I held the intention to reclaim my sense of joie de vivre. Later I watched the beautiful fireworks display over the ocean at Santa Barbara. At the labyrinth, I was given a special prayer to say at midnight. It was perfect to recite while couples kissed at midnight. I had something to do even though I still shed many tears.

The next New Year's Eve I decided to make a list of what I was letting go of as the year changed. Here's what I wrote:

1. Being married.
2. A poverty mentality.
3. Deep grieving.
4. Procrastination.

Ending the year I decided to also do a process I had learned in a healing course. It is an exercise to release things that are impeding your wholeness. Self-love and peace were the first things to review. I committed to release a bad body image, technological challenges, and holding on to my past. The next consideration was what kept me from realizing my dreams. My give away was holding on to the past and a lack of imagination. What kept me from having harmony within my family was the next question to ponder. I shed the expectations of how my family members should be and act around me. Last I gave away what was keeping me from accepting movement and change in my life. I intended to release wanting things to be different, discomfort with the unknown, resentment, and fear. I then looked at what I wanted to experience in my life: prosperity, abundance, my book written and published, completion of the addition on my home in Greece, and to learn more about the harp.

A woman who lost her husband had to cope with the fact that their wedding anniversary was on New Year's Day. She chose to face the challenging day head on by having an open house. She had a buffet table and put out pictures of her husband as a tribute to him and encouraged people to share memories of him.

If we waited to celebrate holidays until our lives were going great not many of us would be celebrating. It is a time to celebrate even when you are in the darkness. **Even in your sorrow you can open to the light.**

Anniversaries

There are different kinds of anniversaries that can trigger a riptide. It can be the anniversary of when your loved one got ill, when they died, a wedding or a birthday. These are dates that you can prepare for ahead of time just like the holiday season. Again, having a plan is a huge help.

The first one I had to cope with happened about a month after Frank died. It would have been our twenty-ninth wedding anniversary. Dear friends brought me to Denmark for a reunion. This group of friends met in the '70s while living in New Jersey and meet up every three years as now we are spread around the planet. None of these special cohorts could attend his celebration of life so I planned a toast to Frank and an opportunity to share wonderful memories of him. I was able to speak at this celebration of the man I had loved for so many years. We all laughed and cried together. We found the perfect wine to share; a large bottle with the label "Big Frank's Great Red." Frank was a big man. It was good to be held in the arms and presence of such friends on this difficult day.

The next wedding anniversary I took the day off from work. I planted a beautiful rose bush named Sheer Bliss with an exquisite fragrance in a pot outside my apartment in Santa Barbara. Frank and I loved picnics so I made a simple one of cheese, a baguette of French bread, and a bottle of good champagne, and ate this feast while sitting on my living room floor. I lit candles and reread some of our love letters that were written in 1976. Some were so poignant. In one of them when we were having no success getting pregnant, I could see his strong faith in his words. He wrote that there is a Divine plan whether we understand it or not. He said the same words on the tape he made me after he was diagnosed with cancer. Some in the *Growing Through Loss* course couldn't believe I could do what I did on such a difficult day. I told them I knew I was going to be sad no matter what I did so I decided to do it with some style.

On the first anniversary of Frank's death or graduation into spirit, I was in Greece taking care of my home. Dear friends helped me get through this day. We planted an oak tree behind my house. It was a sapling that they grew from an acorn. We went to my favorite tiny church right on the sea. Waves were crashing on the walls as we lit fifty-one candles, one for every year he lived, filling the small chapel with light. It was powerful. This was the same church Jane lit candles for Frank the day he died. That night John, Jane's husband, prepared a special Mexican dinner complete with champagne. Their son Gabriel, Jane, and I made brownies. We sang songs Frank loved like, "It's hard to be humble when you are perfect in every way." We had fun and held the idea it was a spiritual anniversary party for Frank's passing.

On the second anniversary of my loss I wrote this entry in my journal:

> *Today is the second anniversary of Frank's death. I spent time alone with my memories and let go a balloon into the air to Frank. It is easier this year, but still a difficult day. At least my memories are more the beautiful ones than the painful ones this time round.*

On the anniversary of his wife's death, Bill, a friend of mine, had me go with him to the cemetery for a picnic. He shared memories of his beloved of fifty years of marriage and we cried and laughed. It was a true communion.

Frank's birthday proved to be another riptide. I knew it would be difficult without some preparation and structure. I kept hearing and seeing the echo that ritual can help with loss. I decided to use ritual for getting through Frank's upcoming birthday. I began the day with a good cup of coffee and sat and thanked God for Frank's life. I also thanked his mom and dad for bringing him into the world. I treated myself to a massage. I bought a piece of chocolate cheesecake which was Frank's favorite. I was crying as the woman cut and wrapped it. I explained my tears. She shared that she had lost her father to cancer five years before. At home I planted a rose bush and listened to Frank's favorite music: *Evita, Chariots of Fire,* and music from *The Thornbirds,* and I sobbed.

I made a memorial candle. Taking a tall candle and putting it in a clear glass, I glued photos of Frank all around and sealed it. It was to be lit on holidays and birthdays. It was a ritual making it and burning it each time.

My dear sister sent me six long-stemmed roses. "In celebration of Frank's birthday – God's gift to you Gail" is what she wrote on the card. Knowing it would be a rough day, I also got a call from South Africa from Helen and Peter, my cheerleaders. My friend Rose remembers every year to connect with me on his birthday.

My birthday was also difficult. Frank had always made my birthday special. Now it was up to me to carry on that tradition. I planned a picnic on the beach with a friend. We took bubbles to blow and had sandwiches and raspberries, which I love. It was a beautiful day of mist and sun. We flew kites and talked deeply. That night I fixed a special meal for myself. I had lobster, asparagus, and champagne. I set the table with my best china, crystal and silverware. I lit fifty-two tea candles and put them on a small table covered with a lovely white cloth. It was wonderful. As I lit each candle I connected with that specific year of my age. Only a few years I couldn't recall something that happened. So many beautiful memories surfaced. I sat there sipping my champagne watching the candles flicker. Some flames flashed wildly while others were pretty stable, like the different years. I noted that thirty-four of the fifty-two years I'd lived, Frank had been in my life. He only got to fifty-one years here on this earth.

The anniversary of the diagnosis was horrible. I relived the shock, terror, and was bombarded with recalled dreadful conversations. I was told to get his affairs in order ASAP; the worst case scenario could be he had two weeks to live. To help my healing on the anniversary of this tragic day, I arranged to have a massage and held the intention to release the trauma. I wanted to be present and not reliving all the horrors. So much fear came up during the session and extreme sadness. I took a walk on the beach later and bought myself some flowers.

Unexpected Riptides

I also had unexpected riptides with strong undertows that pulled me under, like the first time I went as a single to a party filled with couples. Another time I convinced myself to go to an opera on my own and the woman sitting next to me said, "You're not alone are you?" in an incredulous tone. STAB!

Paying the income taxes after Frank's death was very difficult. This was something he had always handled. I was raw as I had to retrace all the doctor appointments and each prescription to claim as deductions. I had such a strong reaction; it leveled me. I felt like I was going to pass out. I could hardly breathe. It was like a tidal wave hit me. Looking at the last year's daily calendar with the specific events was deeply painful.

This exact week a year before, he had two surgeries. His arm broke sleeping on it because of a big tumor in the bone. They announced another tumor was in his lung. The vena cava closed off and they put a stent in it. He had a dramatic and scary reaction to the anesthetic. Then his heart went out of rhythm. It was a nightmare. I again feel the tiredness and terror I experienced last year. I wonder when the emotional rollercoaster will end.

Like a swimmer struggling to break free from swirling waters with strong undercurrents, I had to look at all the funeral expenses, selling most of our belongings, and moving expenses. Doing the taxes almost a year after he died forced me to open all those doors again. It was a process that ripped the Band-Aid® off my wounded being. I tuned into my breath, making sure I was breathing slow and deep. I took a walk around the block to try to rebalance my thoughts and mind.

Another time I was working on legal work to get a piece of property transferred into my name. I had to send in both Frank's death certificate and our marriage license. I stood in my apartment with one in each hand. One hand held so much joy and happiness while my other hand held such sadness and pain. I cried and cried. Each paper represented such a major turning point in my life. I brought both hands and papers to my heart and breathed in peace and exhaled sorrow.

While in mourning, I took a trip with friends to the mountains. It was renewing and relaxing until we went into several antique stores. I have always loved antiques since I was twelve. It was tough because I saw so many things like the pieces I'd had to sell or just let go of when Frank died. It brought up how overnight I had to sort through our things and downsize so dramatically while I was so distraught. I decided to focus on the joy that my things were giving others and I was blessed to have had them for a period of time. Shifting my thoughts shifted my feelings. It sometimes shocked me which things would underline my loss.

I knew taking off my wedding ring would be very difficult. I had only taken it off once in nearly thirty years when I had to go to the hospital and then Frank put it back on my finger immediately when I returned home. I decided to create a ritual around this monumental act. I went to a lovely hot spring north of Santa Barbara alone. It was a beautiful sunny day; new growth was sprouting up on the landscape and the promise of spring was in the air. The hills Frank loved so much were tinted green. The name of the hot tub was Enchantment. It was set back in the trees and very private. I took rose oil with me as it prepares one for moving forward and aids in grief, according to aromatherapy, and lit some candles to light my way in the labyrinth of grief. I was advancing with my bereavement work, but still living it, still purifying, and healing. I spoke to Frank. I told him that we would always be one, eternally, whether I had a ring on my finger or not. In taking it off I was saying YES to life. I was deciding consciously not to cling to what was, but to look forward and live. I told him I was open to my present and my future. Of course, I was also proclaiming these intentions to myself as well. I cried and then I took my wedding band from my finger and placed it on a gold chain with his wedding ring and both of our baby rings. They formed rings within rings, circles within circles. I knew I couldn't just haphazardly take my ring off and my ritual helped make it be more heartfelt and sacred.

Twice the sight of other men launched a riptide. I saw a tall gray haired man in a parking lot and my heart skipped a beat... it could have been "my" Frank. The second situation was a much stronger tsunami. It was the second New Year's Eve on my own. I experienced a mixture of feelings as I was shook to my core and all the settled sediments surfaced, even ones I wasn't aware of. I saw a man with a very similar physique to Frank's at a New Year's Eve meditation in Santa Barbara. I hadn't seen anyone with a similar body since he died twenty months before. He had a rare body type: six foot 6-inches and broad shoulders. The man at the gathering had Frank's body, even down to the large hands and feet. He sat right at my feet in the circle. I couldn't get over the reaction I had in my body. I wanted to touch him. Not really him, but Frank. He had his shoes off and he had happy dancing feet also like Frank. He kept rubbing his girlfriend's shoulders and back and gazing intently into her eyes. Oh, my God. I could feel and remember those touches and looks of adoration and I yearned. Tears flowed gently down my face. I later spoke to him and said how much his body type was like my late husband's and we shared a needed hug. I processed this riptide in my EMDR session and with an energy session with Peter.

Another profoundly deep and difficult passage was spreading Frank's ashes. I was attending a women's retreat on Maui and it was the humpback whales calving season. We were going to go by boat to see the mother whales and their babies. Frank loved baby animals; I knew this would be an ideal opportunity to release his ashes. I poured them gently into the water at the back of the boat surrounded and supported by good friends. As I finished the captain came on the loud speaker and said he forgot to tell us that they call the whales "gentle giants." As so many people referred to Frank as a gentle giant, I knew what I had done was perfect.

Expect that certain events will give you emotional whiplash. You will also be surprised at what will trigger such profound reactions in your mind, emotions, and body. Prepare for those you anticipate and remember the tools you have learned to help when you are caught off guard. Notice in many of my examples that I felt better once I reframed the situation to something even a bit more positive.

In hospice we recommended creating a box with quotes of encouragement and words from caring and comforting friends and family. Include tissues and anything else that would help you through the tough situations. **Allow your heart to stay open; remember all these experiences are opportunities for deeper healing.**

Heartfelt Suggestions

Now it is time to go to a quiet place where you can take some time for yourself. Bring a notebook and pen. Place your hand over your heart and close your eyes. Take several slow deep breaths down into your lower belly. Allow your breath to guide you to the peaceful place within your heart. Now open your eyes and begin reading and reflect on the suggestions. This is part of your conscious mourning and it is sacred work.

1. Make a list of the riptides you can expect.

2. Begin creating a tentative plan for each ahead of time.

3. How can you do your holidays differently to make them even a bit easier? Don't expect too much of yourself while grieving.

4. Are there any rituals that could help you get through the riptides in your current life?

5. Are there ways you can honor your loved one at these times?

CHAPTER SEVEN

RE-CREATION: *Self-Recovery and Discovery*

YOU HAVE BEEN BROKEN APART. How do you begin to put the scattered pieces of the puzzle you call life together again? Bit by bit a new picture will take form as you integrate your loss into your life and your being. Transformation will take time and patience, but your efforts are necessary. Now let's concentrate on rebuilding and restoring – a re-creation of a new life if you will.

A drop in self-esteem is a common side effect with a major loss. In a study in self-esteem using a scale of 100, it was found that an average person's self-esteem is in the 70s and generally a bereaved person's registers in the teens. Understanding the impact of grief on your self-esteem may help you find ways of coping.

Grief left me battered, depleted, and deflated. I felt like a shadow of my former self and I'm not referring to my weight. With my underpinnings pulled out from under me I was not as confident as I had been before Frank's passing. I needed to rebuild myself, reclaim my character and spirit. At first I struggled just to survive and get through my days and nights. I grasped for any anchor to keep me steady. Through the mourning process, you tend to develop new strengths and abilities by default, but I decided to ultimately transcend, not just survive. There had to be something good come out of this experience. Today when I review my life and look for periods of profound growth, I realize that I normally expand and stretch during my challenging experiences. You have the opportunity for survival, resilience, and transcendence as you navigate the rough waters of grief.

You are in the process of re-creation. The origin of the word recreation is restoration to health from *recreare* which is Latin. It means to create anew and to restore. I think of this place of re-creation as the shoreline between what you have known and the unknown that is still forming. The beach is that narrow band of equilibrium where the old you meets the emerging you. This is a sacred space of great potential and it is filled with transcendent energy. You must release the tendency to grasp what was and not cling to your past. You are better served if you become a beachcomber for a while as the shore is a place of rebirth. It is a place where you can shed patterns and pain that don't serve your highest good. It is a place where you can choose a new design, a new way of being. The ocean is a prime example of flexibility and resilience. Whenever I have been troubled the ocean has given me balance and a better perspective.

On the Native American medicine wheel, which is a framework to connect with yourself and the infinite, the direction of west is important during grief. It is marked by unlimited fluidity and the ability to cleanse, nurture, heal, and purify like the sea. The west is also associated with fall, the time of harvesting and letting go.

I desired to bring honoring, some style, sacredness, soulfulness, heart, and beauty into the equation during my rite of passage, my healing. Anything can be taken to the level of art, even mourning. Let your heart guide you: it knows the way.

When you become still and tune within, what does your heart tell you? Don't spend your time and energy analyzing and explaining why you are where you are. Best not to just sit on the shore; it is better to make some movement. Even a small step forward will suffice. Do something that makes you feel better, for a start. If you do something you love this will be uplifting. If you haven't made the list of things that make you feel good that I mentioned earlier, now is an excellent time to begin brainstorming and do this exercise. Begin by recalling what has made you feel good in the past. I set the goal to do at least one of the items on my list per week. Feed your soul; do something you love. One week I noted that I had an ice cream, listened to music, and set up a massage for myself.

I know you have been berating yourself for the things you are struggling to accomplish. Now I want you to acknowledge what you have done well considering the circumstances. Remember to take into consideration your response-ability at this juncture in your journey.

Look to your past for what helped you gain courage and what helped you to stabilize in other situations. I observed times when I had been strong and capable, and I searched for times I had been resilient. This was part of remembering and recapturing who I was. Look at the word re-member to put the parts back together. Sometimes I felt like I was on an archeological dig as I searched for a stronger and confident me. I began to reclaim the parts of me that grief had eclipsed and I documented all these reclamations in my journal.

While I did this kind of inner work I needed to find respite in solitude. I kept space for my grief, knowing how important it was to do my work and not avoid my mourning journey. I didn't over-schedule myself with too many things to do which had been my prior pattern. I knew I was in an important period of self-recovery and discovery. I wanted to touch base as often as possible with that wise spark within my heart. I made it a priority to regularly focus my attention inward because at this time I knew that *my* life was at stake. I wanted to put the lost pieces of myself back into the picture of my emerging new life.

Show up for yourself and practice being still when you are overwhelmed. Sit down, stop, and breathe. It is all right to occasionally disappoint people when your current needs aren't a match to what they think is best for you. You might turn down an invitation to nurture your soul in a different way. Go within to align with your true self and the Inner Wise One in your heart, your inner knowing. This is where your true essence resides. This is the home of your inner voice or intuition and guidance. This is your *Resilient Heart*® which has an innate transcendent nature. Guidance from this source will lead you to a place of wholeness and authenticity.

Making that connection results in peace and often happiness. Rumi, the poet, spoke for that preciousness in your heart: *"I am the pure awareness within your heart, with you during joy and celebration, suffering and despair."*

From a place of balance you will find more clarity and can connect to that pure awareness within your heart. One day I noticed the saying "Life can be a fine balancing act," which was printed on a South African wine label. The logo was an elephant precariously balanced on a small box with the words Happy Equilibrium. I told you that I find messages everywhere. It is time to rebalance, rejuvenate, rebuild, and replenish. There are many ways to do this. If one suggestion doesn't work for you go to another.

Inspiration

I created a sanctuary for my healing in my apartment. I bought a bouquet of fresh flowers weekly from the grocery store. I courted myself and attempted to take care of me as I would a precious friend. I was befriending Gail on a deeper and more conscious level.

I decided to surround myself with things that would inspire and uplift me. I suggest you do the same. I don't care if you only have a tiny room or a corner of a room to call your own. Create a haven for solace and encouragement. I designed a comfortable place that would invite me to be still, to write in my journal, to process, to pray, cry, meditate, and would inspire my healing. I gathered books that have fed my soul: *Gift from the Sea* by Anne Morrow Lindberg; *Illustrated Rumi* by Michael Green and Coleman Barks; and *The Prophet* by Kahlil Gibran. I even found a copy of *The Little Engine That Could*, which was my favorite childhood book. "I think I can" was what the little engine repeated over and over as he struggled up the mountain – a good mantra, if you will, for what I was going through at the time. I added other books as I found appropriate ones. I chose music that I loved and would relax me. Quotes that moved me and gave me guidance were gathered. *Angel Blessings, Cards of Sacred Guidance and Inspiration* by Kimberly Marooney came into my life and were included in my sanctuary. I had pictures and artwork that inspired me to create courage as well as being aesthetically pleasing. All of these things were soul food. I searched for poetry that would help me during this time of transition and transformation. A candle was important to add to my healing environment. I also had to have a dragonfly, as it was a family symbol for holding on. I put an image of a Phoenix rising that I drew to guide me to "mourning" glory. I bought a gorgeous purple wine glass to drink my water in style.

My new mascot, a small stuffed rabbit, "Be bwave wittle wabbit, be bwave," sat on my desk. He reminded me to be courageous and resilient. He still does.

Start thinking what you want in your sanctuary. My cat, Rumi, hung out wherever I was, so he was in my sanctuary. He always knew when I needed a cuddle and a purr. I bought an orchid plant as they are the flower with the highest energy and are very healing in a room. Collecting whimsical things made me smile. You can also train yourself to look at your day for inspiration. I set the intention to look for things that touched my heart or encouraged me. Just asking the questions prompts you to look for things that move, inspire, and touch your heart. It might be the lyrics of a song, an opening flower, the sight of a shooting star or a baby kitten. I recall hearing "set me free to rise up from the ashes," in a song on the radio and was filled with boldness.

Music

In the chapter *Releasing* I shared how powerful it was in my healing to do sound work. I also explained how music helped me to go into a deep level of consciousness while receiving EMDR work. Research has shown that music affects your biology either enhancing or disturbing wholeness. It can soothe or create anxiety depending on what you listen to. I suggest you use it consciously to entrain to peace. Think of any particular music that has relaxed you in the past and play it. Your heart rate, pulse, and respiration can all be affected by sound. Think of your reaction to hearing chalk screeching across a blackboard; it pierces your being. Then consider listening to a piece of music like *Moonlight Sonata* or Pachelbel's *Canon*. Just thinking about these different sounds causes repercussions within your body.

When I give a massage or energy session, I normally play restful music but with no words. Words tend to pull you into your mind and the left side of your brain. When I wasn't trying to relax deeply, but rather needed encouragement to cheer me on I tried to find the perfect song. When I was working on handling all the bureaucratic tasks, I put on the song *Taking Care of Business*. Music can provide affirmation for our feelings.

Sometimes I played upbeat music to bring me up and other times I listened to music that mirrored what I was feeling. If I just wanted a pity party and to cry, I would choose songs that had meaning for Frank and me. Notice I was doing the orchestrating consciously, at times anyway. The first time I took a holiday on my own I was having bouillabaisse by the sea in southern France. I had to build myself up to sit there solo. And what music streams out of the restaurant but our song *More*, and it was being sung in English! I didn't arrange that, but perhaps Frank did.

While in France I learned about the Cluny Abbey. They had a hospice in the eleventh century that used prescriptive music including chants to unbind the spirit from the body to help people transition smoothly during death. It was a beautiful confirmation to learn this as there was a harpist playing at Frank's transition. He did die with a huge smile and with such peace. This fueled my determination to play the harp for others at their time to leave their earth-suit. When I did begin to play the harp for the dying, I prayed that the music would be an instrument of peace and comfort mentally, emotionally, physically, and spiritually. One occasion that I took the harp with me to the *Growing Through Loss* course, many cried as I played, hopefully not because it was so terrible. Actually many thanked me after the gathering. I told them I was asking for healing energy to flow to them no matter what strings I plucked. I figure if music could help one transition at death, why couldn't it help me and others transition back into life after the death of a loved one?

I read of a group in Illinois called *Healing Harps*. People with Cerebral Palsy and Multiple Sclerosis are finding that they are healing when they play the harp. The music gives an acoustic massage as the vibrations enter the body. The music counters the negative effects on the immune system. They are creating significant improvements in their health. I found a freedom while playing the harp and it relaxed me deeply.

I found another motivation to continue my music lessons. I attended a workshop with Andrew Harvey and he spoke of the power of music. He said that opera and some music can bring on an orgasmic experience. I told my sister and we laughed as I recommitted to improving my playing with more practice with gusto.

> *I continued my "feed my soul" campaign. I went to a concert; the live music is helping me heal. I relaxed my body and let the sound vibrations flow through me. The singer sang my favorite aria from Puccini and Ave Maria which we had played at our wedding. They sang one song that pierced me: "Have Yourself a Merry Little Christmas" and the part "We shall all draw together if the fates allow" grabbed my heart. They didn't allow.*

A year after Frank left his earth-suit, I went to a symphony of Beethoven's *Missa Solemnis*. It was Mother's Day. I held the intention that the Divine Mother was rebirthing me through the music. I had incredible feelings as heat filled each of my energy centers or chakras. There was intense heat in back of my heart area like I had felt in a session with Peter and during a meditation I did on the anniversary of Frank's passing.

182

I later wrote in my journal:

> *I feel I am less dense. I aim to be hollow, emptied of this grief like a flute. Then peace and joy will be able to flow through me like beautiful music.*

Art

"At the deepest level, the creative process and the healing process arise from a single source." ~ Dr. Rachel Naomi Remen

Art has been an important part of my life since childhood. I enjoy viewing lovely artwork and creating art. Going to an art museum or gallery has always lifted my spirits and filled my heart with joy and inspiration. I definitely needed uplifting and inspiration during this time and looked to art to aid me in my healing process.

I recalled a picture a dear friend had on her wall that moved me. I contacted her and she said it was a piece of the painting *The Mystical Boat* by Odilon Redon. She found it in the book *The Gaze of Love* by Sister Wendy Beckett. Christina sent a copy of it to me. The painting depicts a woman sitting in a blue sailboat with a brilliant yellow-gold sail. There is a companion in the boat, but subtly seen. The message that accompanied the painting in the book was perfect for me. It said two are there because the mystic heart is never alone. It describes the companion as an angel or God who is always present and guiding if we can surrender.

This description helped me as I felt like I was adrift on a boat with no means to control what happened to Frank's and my life. I was reminded to surrender to my circumstances. Allow without resistance. I needed reminding often.

Two other artistic images came into my possession while I was grieving. I was gifted with an exquisite antique Russian icon of Mother Mary and Christ as a baby. The other was also a thoughtful present. It came from one of my hospice patients and was a lovely magazine image of Mary Magdalene holding an egg. Both of these sacred images fanned my faith during the troubled dark night of my soul. I looked at the egg as a symbol of birth, renewal, and hope.

All of the artwork I chose to surround me reminded me that I was not really alone, but just on my own. What images can you collect to uplift your spirit? You can find them in magazines or a book; it need not be a piece of fine art. Looking at a Monet painting moves me to tears and stirs my soul. Needless to say I don't own one, but I can see them in a book or in a museum. Find something for your sense of sight that can aid in your transformational process. These are affirmations for your eyes.

Often the motivation for great works of art, music, dance, and theater is loss. Go to an art museum with the intent to look for images depicting grief and you will find many. Andrea Bayer, the curator of European painting at the Metropolitan Museum of Art in New York City, traced her process of mourning though paintings hanging in the museum. She was grieving the death of both of her parents within a year. You can watch a video of the pictures she chose to represent her pain at: www.metmuseum.org/connections/grief#/Feature/.

Not only can you encourage your healing by absorbing with your eyes the images of others' art or photography, you can also create your own. The American Art Therapy Association's Mission Statement expresses the healing possibilities of the creative process: "The creative process involved in the making of art is healing and life enhancing." In hospice we encouraged the grieving children to draw or paint their difficult emotions. Using expressive arts for healing isn't reserved just for children. At any age sometimes there just aren't words to express what you are deeply feeling.

I decided to take a course in expressing your emotions through art. I had taught drawing and painting, but not with this focus that I now wanted. The course I found was called *Healing Through Art* and was offered by Santa Barbara's adult education. The teacher explained that art has been shown to help heal and lift the spirits of participants. He said we all are healing from something and that art isn't all hearts and flowers; it can express negative and difficult feelings. It is a journey that isn't always fun, but it can be a good focus when life falls apart.

In the first class, the instructor read a poem which mentioned gateways through the eyes. I did a simple watercolor on a narrow vertical piece of paper of a large eye with tears flowing down to a pool which then rose upward like a fountain. My intention was to depict life-giving waters created from the tears of grief. The instructor usually played some soothing music and the session began with a meditation to get us in touch with the feelings we wanted to paint. With eyes closed, we took several slow deep breaths to center, closed the door to outer distractions, and became present with ourselves. Think what a gift it is when someone gives you their undivided attention, their presence. We were reminded to give this precious gift to ourselves and dive within and express from there.

I love a concept held in Bali. They consider everyone is an artist, but perhaps in different mediums. I agree with the Balinese. As a child you freely expressed with paint and pencil and weren't concerned if you knew how to do it "right." You don't even need to know how to draw or to paint. If your expressions tend to look like a small child's, so be it.

At times it is difficult to even put a label on what you are experiencing. If this happens, just begin by choosing a color that best represents the sensations. Remember: this is not about being a great artist – this is to express your grief. Use the process as an outlet for your painful emotions. The intent is the process, not the end result. You need not share what you do with anyone. I added doodles, scribbles, stick figures, and rough sketches in my journal as well as doing separate images on sheets of paper. Some were quick sketches on notebook paper and others were on a sheet of watercolor paper. They are cathartic renderings, not attempts to make great art.

I keep crayons, watercolors, colored pens, scissors, and glue near my journal as well as pencils, paper and pens. I suggest you gather some supplies to make it easy to express your feelings in the spur of the moment. Choose the art materials that would invite you to play with them. I bought luscious rich pastel crayons in incredible and tantalizing hues.

I cut images out of magazines for collages and put them in a file. One collage I designed depicted winter and bareness to represent this phase of my life. I wrote on the back: "How do I get my bearings back in this strange and barren landscape of my soul?" You can add words and colors on top of a collage or intertwine them as well. There are no rules here. Let your inner little child out to speak through image, color, shape, line, and texture.

Let your heart guide you rather than your head. Your head can't figure it all out anyway, so allow your heart to guide you. Stay with your feelings, not your thoughts. You may gather new and important information from within by connecting to your Inner Wise One. I often feel like I lose myself while doing artwork and invariably then truly find ME. Using art as a way to express can be very meditative. Your intention is not to make a lovely picture, but to communicate the truth of where you are or to discover what you truly are feeling.

The images you make might be wild, even ugly and dark, but it doesn't matter if they are authentic. Turn off your inner critic. You can even close your eyes when you put your first marks or lines on your paper if that makes it easier. I sometimes use my non-dominant hand to draw. What that does is makes you switch to your right brain out of your logical left brain and tends to free you from trying to be so perfect. I often feel that I go into a meditative state when doing something creative. I can get in touch with my feelings and then give them a voice through my art.

Upon completion of a project ask what your visual expression is saying. Do not invite your inner critic to make comments. You aren't analyzing how you drew or painted, but what you see in what you created. Listen for your heart to speak, not your mind for insight and Inner-Prizes. Write your responses on the back of your picture or on the opposite page of your journal and date it.

I poured out emotions through line and color. In one of my six journals of mourning I wrote:

> *I am getting ideas for a collage or painting. I can see Aphrodite or Venus born on the waves of the ocean of grief. Another image is the Phoenix rising from the fire and ashes of what was. A baby could represent new birth. I will work with these ideas.*

Another entry:

> *These images are in my head: dancing with my shadow, fragments regrouping, splintered parts unclaimed and hidden becoming whole like a puzzle or a magnet drawing things back. I am playing with combining a picture of my beach rose, the purple heart, and white balloons for a print.*

At one point I captured my anger with an ink drawing of a tightly clenched fist. Behind it is an outstretched hand with energy lines streaming from the fingertips. There are notes to paint the gripping fist red and the other hand in healthy glowing colors. I noted at the top that at the time I was experiencing tightness in my fingers and hands. I scrawled the words *Anger* and *Frustration* across the top of the lined notebook page. I listed the triggers for my anger: "Can't find the will; Frank's death; Frank not leaving files more orderly; hospital situations, and insurance company." On another page I've drawn a woman with one hand at her throat, head tilted forward with tears flowing down her face and dropping into a small container. Underneath the sketch are lots of words: "Sorrows Sojourn; the heart is raw and vulnerable; tears, the glistening gems of grief; the portal of pain; sleep, the temporary balm; the naked tears of grief cleansing my soul; drops of sadness; what color is grief ?; blessed memories please fill my longing and heal my wounded heart. Where's the lullaby to soothe my spirit and ease this searing pain?" On a half piece of typing paper I did a small image of a woman slumped over, head down on her hand at a table. I wrote *Despair* at the top of the page.

Looking over the drawings and sketches I made that document my mourning journey, I note that quite a few are in a circle. These are called mandalas, as I mentioned earlier. The term mandala comes from a Sanskrit word meaning "circle." A circle is a universal symbol and represents wholeness. Roundness is sacred as the most natural shape, according to J.C. Cooper in *An Illustrated Encyclopedia Of Traditional Symbols.* Carl Jung worked with mandalas to observe his and others' transformations. He felt that drawing them led to wholeness and healing. They are visual expressions creating order by constructing a center and a concentric arrangement. Working with them leads to stability and inner peace. They have been used as a meditative focus in Tibetan Buddhism and in the Western traditions as well. Hildegard of Bingen, an abbess of a Benedictine Abbey eight hundred years ago, illustrated her visions often in the form of a mandala.

At times individuals instinctively draw them, but you can guide the process by starting with a circle on a paper. You can trace a saucer or a dinner plate as your template and go from there. Center yourself by bringing your awareness to your breath and then ask your heart what to express. Once you realize what your intention is in creating your mandala, brainstorm for any symbols, colors, numbers you might want to incorporate. You might prefer to just begin and see what happens without a plan. Remember: you can't make a mistake. A friend of mine calls this spontaneous approach "creative windsurfing," as you let the winds take you where they may. Your subconscious is the artist.

In the chapter *Relating*, I described the mandala I created to express the support I felt from others. I painted another one to depict holding or hanging on. I put a picture of a ceramic angel pin in the center. I told you how she repeatedly broke while Frank was ill and I kept gluing her together. Above her are the words HOLD FAST. Around the outer edge are eight dragonflies facing inward with their tails breaking out of the large circle. Recall the dragonfly is a symbol to me of resilience, tenacity, and holding on. I researched the meaning of eight after I drew this. Eight represents regeneration, resurrection, rebirth, eternity, and perfect rhythm.

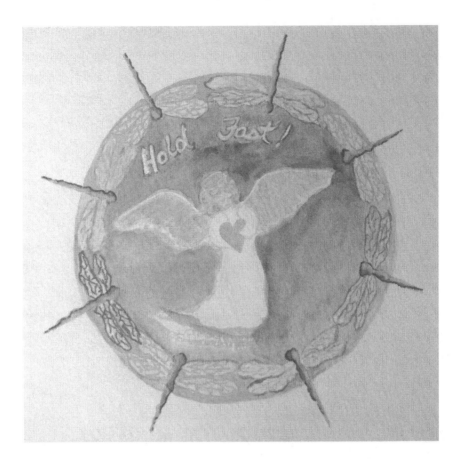

I orchestrated transcendence in another mandala. A Phoenix is flying upward in the center. You view it looking down on it and it seems to be flying up toward you. It is enclosed by a triangle representing a doorway to birth or rebirth. The outer rim of the circle is composed of a ring of fire. This symbol of the Phoenix rising from its ashes was an important inspiration during my mourning journey. You can see other art I created to express my grief on my website: GailSaunders.com.

Another idea is to make a mask and paint your grief on it using symbols and colors that represent what you are experiencing.

Drawing and painting helped me bring order to transcend the chaos of my grief. I often felt empowered after finishing a visual expression of my emotions, not because of how it turned out, but because of the process of making it. I drew images from my dreams, visions, and imagination, and, of course, from my emotions that were screaming for a voice, for expression. I suggest you do the same.

Life-Affirming Rituals

"Such rituals are like candles in the window, dispelling a bit of grief's dark night while casting light on a path that leads to hope and healing." ~ Mera Cossy Corlett, M.Div., from article in the Oates Journal 2011, *A Lipstick, a Ribbon and Grey Clay: Creating Grief Rituals for Children*.

I have referred to several rituals or ceremonies that I have created to help me integrate my loss. The ritual in the hot springs to remove my wedding ring is a good example. I have used rituals to honor important crossroads or events in my life, so naturally I turned to them to aid me at this major junction.

When you create a ritual you are outwardly expressing what is happening within. Just as the body needs food, so our souls need to be nurtured by rituals that give form and substance to the longings and feelings of your heart and soul. They are orchestrated actions that aid in shifting perception and healing. They can bring reverence, sacredness, and honor to the significant signposts in life. You already grace your life with rituals: anniversaries, graduations, weddings, funerals, and baby christenings, to name a few. It is also possible to formulate a very personal ritual for the crucial events in your life. I know my willingness to dive into my pain and work with it in ways like ritual enabled me to begin to experience joy again. They can help you to do the same.

I used balloons as one form of ritual. When my mom died in 1992, at the graveside there were seven of us and we each released a different color balloon with the thought of sending a rainbow of love to her. I took balloons to the children's grief group that I co-facilitated for hospice and they wrote messages to their loved one on the balloon with magic markers and we let them go. The day Frank died I told our friends and family to release a balloon for him. Balloons were sent up to him all around the world. Later they each said how perfect it was, they had something they could do immediately. That night Velvet and I bought lots of balloons and we stood on the deck under the stars. We released them and toasted Frank at his graduation from this life with champagne. As they rose they blended with the stars. Later at the celebration of Frank's life in a park on a hillside with views of the mountains in Santa Barbara, we released white balloons that cascaded across the sky. I always cut the string off so no bird will get caught up in it and use only biodegradable balloons.

I decided to share this idea with one of my grief support groups and ordered a balloon for each member. I shared at the gathering how special balloons have been for me. I got some wonderful feedback about the balloons the following week. Bill saw two eagles when he let his go with a message to his departed wife and then he had a beautiful dream about it that night. One woman kept her balloon. Another said hers got away in the school bathroom and she got a good laugh. One woman's father died that week at the age of ninety-three. The family got ninety-three balloons for his funeral. Another person was going to take hers to a mountain top and let it go, but her grandson broke it. Her children bought her another. One tied hers to her dog's collar and she laughed and laughed. Several said they couldn't let theirs go. I got several personal thank you notes for sharing this ritual.

Two years after Frank died I created a ritual to put away some of the many photos I had of him around my small apartment. There were about twenty. I decided to narrow the count down to two as he lives in my heart. I purchased a beautiful box in which to put the others. I decided to add all the cards and love letters he wrote as well into the box. I lit candles and put on a collection of Frank's favorite music. I reread many of the cards and letters and I naturally cried, but I made it a sacred and honored event. I was also saying I was not clinging to my past, but rather becoming open to moving forward toward my future.

In my sister's neighborhood they purchase a tree for a family who has lost a loved one. They gather and plant the tree in that family's yard in support, creating a loving community.

During the second year of my mourning I planned a trip back to Santa Cruz where Frank died. My intention was to bring about some closure by visiting the hospital where he died and to go to the place we had lived at the time. I had a five hour drive from Santa Barbara, so I took some inspiring music, bought a single purple iris and put it in a water bottle in the car, and headed north. I went to the hospital first. His room number was 2508. The door was closed so I stood there and prayed. I didn't go in and ask if I could touch the bed; I behaved myself. I did go to the chapel and stood a long time in front of the statue of Christ with His hand raised in blessing. I felt such intense energy as I knelt and prayed in front of the metal cross on the altar and gazed at the rough-hewn stained glass. I then stood in the streaming colors of light and let them penetrate me.

Next I drove to Happy Valley Road where we had lived. Lots of memories flooded my mind. The redwoods felt good and comforting, and I breathed in the earthy smells. I visited my neighbor. We dug up a small cluster of tiny redwoods. It is interesting how they grow. Their roots intertwine and are quite shallow depending on community to earth and anchor. I decided they were a perfect symbol of the human family needing each other for support and balance. Driving home I felt high on life. I had good music playing (Winston Marsalis, as a matter of fact), sunshine, the beautiful iris in the water bottle, and the smell of the redwoods permeated the car. I saw nine hawks as I drove. I was glad I had orchestrated this weekend filled with ritual, laughter, tears, and revisiting.

Rituals can add grace to coping with change and bring empowerment during times of transformation. They can elicit clarity and intention as well as transcendence. They can reframe a situation to make it more tolerable and soulful. A ritual can be used as a crucible for your pain, confusion, and loss. A shift is possible with the tool of ritual as you take some control over how you handle your situation. I think of them as touchstones that give order to your chaos while helping integrate loss into your reality.

Faith

"Faith is the strength by which a shattered world shall emerge into the light." ~ Helen Keller

Your world has been shattered by death, and faith in yourself and in something grander than you can help in your restoration.

The word faith is often interchanged with trust, hope, or belief. The Free Dictionary says faith is confident belief in the truth, value, and trustworthiness of a person, idea or thing. It doesn't rest on logical proof.

When thrown into the torrents of grief, my faith in myself and a power greater than myself was profoundly tested. My faith and spiritual beliefs had been a stable force in my life and attempting to hold fast to my faith became a crucial anchor through this time. I am not connected to one specific religion, but I consider myself very spiritual. I would describe my beliefs somewhat like a braid or twisted hair. What resonates in my heart I add to my braid of belief while what doesn't ring true for me I release. I believe in Spirit or God who is unconditional love.

My faith in my own abilities was broken as I floundered in chaos and confusion. I had to rebuild that confidence slowly as I tackled all the responsibilities thrown on me. Facing them one by one with patience ultimately empowered me. I would set small manageable goals with action steps. As a management consultant I had guided large and small organizations to develop corporate goals, and individuals to write personal ones. With the dark eclipse of grief again what I knew how to do became extremely difficult for me to accomplish.

When you take a step, even a tiny step, toward handling what is on your plate, praise yourself. I began looking in the mirror each evening and while looking in my eyes with a hand over my heart, I would tell myself aloud what I appreciated about myself during that day. I didn't have Frank to do that with anymore. We did it every night looking into each other's eyes and placing a hand on the other's heart while sharing what we appreciated about the other that day. A good thing about this practice is that all day you are looking for something to appreciate about yourself rather than scolding yourself for your mistakes. Looking directly into someone's or your own eyes is very intimate. I recommend you try this. At least write your daily appreciation in your journal. This is another example of courting myself and was an important step in rebuilding my self-faith.

Look to your past for times when you had faith in your abilities and you were right. Remember your faith. Don't forget that a

Divine spark resides in your heart center and recalling that can help you begin to move beyond your pain. Reconnecting to our inner flame provides a lifeline to our Source and inner strength.

Sometimes I did wonder where Spirit was. I felt abandoned... but I wasn't. Again, grief eclipsed my conscious connection, but it is always present. On a cloudy day you don't see or feel the sun but you know it is there. I felt the door to God open as I became still in body and mind and surrendered and allowed. If I made the effort to relax physically usually directing my awareness to follow my breath, I felt the loving presence of God and peace could flow into my troubled being. Some days were more difficult than others to relax enough to feel and hear Source. Spirit is always present, but you can't hear Divine guidance if your mind is chattering away. From the silent recesses of your heart call out to your inner wisdom and to God for guidance, and then listen in silence. I learned that although I was on my own I wasn't alone, and you aren't either.

If you have a broken heart, I recommend you give all the pieces to your Source to mend. If you hold and keep the broken pieces of pain, anger, or loneliness they can cut deeply. I am reminded of beach glass that the edges have been smoothed by the sea and they can no longer create cuts when touched. Let whatever you believe in soothe your splintered heart.

I recalled how much support and guidance I received while Frank was ill. In Chapter 4, in the section on fear, I shared how I turned over our problem with no income to God and how my prayers were quickly answered.

Another Divine intervention occurred after Frank died. There was no life insurance but I unexpectedly received $36,000 from his company that paid off the credit card bills by one hundred dollars, which I also shared in Chapter 4.

So when my hope and faith were low I held tight to such experiences. Another touchstone was my vivid vision with Christ a few days before Frank's illness came to the surface. Christ held my face in his hands and told me to know that He was always with me. Even in times when I couldn't make conscious connection with Divine Source I recalled my powerful vision.

The Prayer Before the Crucifix, by Francis of Assisi, helped me when I felt lost and my heart was heavy. "Most High, glorious God, let your light fill the shadows of my heart and grant me, Lord, true faith, certain hope, perfect love, awareness and knowing that I may fulfill your holy will."

Be open to the presence of something grander than yourself. Allow and surrender to your Source even when you don't yet see direction. Decide to move forward toward mourning light.

Learn Something New

I mentioned earlier that I decided at Frank's death to learn to play the harp. As soon as I moved back to Santa Barbara, with synchronicity I found the perfect instructor. I think it was a great idea to begin something new during my time of mourning. It took such concentration and thus gave me a break from my deep grief not only in class but daily as I practiced. Learning something I had been programmed to think I couldn't do helped my bruised self-esteem and gave me focus.

Other grievers I have met learned a new language, took cooking classes, art lessons, and one began salsa dance lessons. They shared how healing it was to open to growth. The intention wasn't necessarily mastery, but the process of exploring something new. All represent taking control and taking steps forward. Recall how important movement is. Brainstorm for ideas you might like to try. What have you put on the back burner of your life that interests you? What makes you feel alive? Pick something and begin by taking the first step.

Gratitude

"But listen to me; for one moment, quit being sad. Hear blessings dropping their blossoms around you. God." ~ Rumi

In every life there are things to be grateful for and you will see them if you are open. What you look for you find! I bought a separate gratitude notebook to record my daily blessings. I decided to look for three things daily that I was thankful for and write them down. I tried not to repeat the entries. I wrote in my journal that it helped me to look for what is good and going well in my life when so much felt so wrong. It made me see how important the little things could be. In the beginning it might have been only that I could leave the apartment, but looking for any blessings directed my focus on the positives in my life.

I continued to do the mirror session each night. I looked into my eyes and said out loud what I appreciated about myself that day with my hand on my heart. The first time I did this I said how proud I was that I was willing to allow my painful feelings to surface. My eyes immediately filled with tears as I acknowledged the courage of this allowance. Acknowledge each of your positive steps in the process of mourning.

Another griever created a gratitude chest with the intention of placing symbols of her blessings to uplift and inspire. She wrote out happy memories, poems, quotes, pictures, stories that inspired her, thank you notes she had received, letters, cards, and appropriate email copies. She said revisiting this box reminded her of the good and powerful qualities she had within.

It empowered her as she reviewed the contents. It was especially helpful on a rough day.

I shared earlier that I made a point to write thank you notes to the many wonderful people who had reached out to us during Frank's illness as well as to me after he died. It took quite a while, but I did write a personal message for each person as this was extremely important to me.

I wrote a letter of gratitude to Frank with the intention to redirect my thoughts to happy memories and away from the painful last four months of his life. For years I told him daily what I appreciated about him. This letter was a summary of the many reasons he was a huge blessing in my life; it was a long letter.

Looking for your blessings and expressing gratitude keeps your heart open and softens the pain. Think about the warmth you feel when a person is appreciative. Know you can give yourself this gift.

Heartfelt Suggestions

Now it is time to go to a quiet place where you can take some time for yourself. Bring a notebook and pen. Place your hand over your heart and close your eyes. Take several slow deep breaths down into your lower belly. Allow your breath to guide you to the peaceful place within your heart. Now open your eyes and begin reading and reflect on the suggestions. This is part of your conscious mourning and it is sacred work.

1. Are you doing things that could make you feel good? Do something that feeds your soul.

2. What in your past helped you to feel balanced? Recall when you felt resilient.

3. Are you creating space in your schedule for your grief work?

4. What books, things, or quotes inspire you and or give you comfort?

5. Have you created a place or sanctuary that is comfortable for you to do your inner work?

6. What inspired you today? What touched your heart?

7. How can you use music as a balancing tool?

8. How could you use art to express your grief or uplift you?

9. What images could depict what you are feeling?

10. What images have inspired you in your past?

11. Can you think of any rituals that could help you to integrate this life passage?

12. How can you build your faith in self?

13. How important is your faith in something greater than yourself? What could you do to strengthen that connection?

14. What new experience can you begin, like a new hobby?

15. Are you looking for things you appreciate daily?

CHAPTER EIGHT

RESILIENCE: "Mourning" Glory

"FIVE, FOUR, THREE, TWO, ONE... BUNGEE!' I did a swan dive off the ten-story bridge where minutes before I couldn't get near the edge of the structure. My intention was to face my fears and take a leap of faith into the next chapter of my life. To my amazement, as I jumped into the void I felt no adrenaline rush, rather the opposite. I was amazingly held in profound peace. Back on the bridge after my jump I proclaimed, "If I can do this, I can do anything. I'm moving to Africa."

This was three years after Frank died. I was feeling a call to a new life as I had weathered my deep grief. I was ready for a new chapter in my life. I had felt strong pulls to Africa, tugs on my heartstrings. Three months before while visiting Namibia and South Africa with friends, I felt at home there. In the past I had listened and followed my heart's callings, but this prompt was monumental; this time I was alone, freeing my hijacked spirit. It was a challenge not to let Frank's death be a stop sign in my life rather than a crossroads.

When I made that proclamation on the bridge to go to Africa, I got out of my way and into the flow of life. The universe stepped in and doors and windows began to open. Someone asked me to live with them for two months before I left California which allowed me to save more than $4,000. I arranged to go to a wonderful guest lodge in Namibia to work in exchange for room and board for three months. While there the owners prompted me to apply for a work permit and offer massage, energy work, and my artwork to the guests. My three months grew to be six profound years filled with such adventures as flying safaris, camping, wild animal sightings, and an archeological dig in a cave that was named after me.

The night before flying to Africa I had a dream. I was going to a formal dance wearing a flowing emerald green taffeta gown. I was barefoot and my hair kept falling free from a French twist. My mother asked me where my date was and I responded, "I don't need one. I will dance and have a great time on my own." In the morning I knew to silence my fears, that I would be fine. I was footloose and fancy-free, following my heart. I decided to say yes to life and to me.

I was more than fine in Africa; I reclaimed my sense of adventure. I completely released my spirit as I felt free and so alive again. I recall thinking, *Welcome back, Gail!* There, in that expansive, wild and raw environment with ancient echoes, I had my renaissance among the oldest dunes in the world. In the birthplace of mankind I found renewed life. Thank God I followed my *Resilient Heart*®!

Broken to Breakthrough

There comes a time to release and let go of the pain. Embrace your tragic loss, integrate it, and stay open to living wholeheartedly again. After all, life is meant for living and you are still here on this earth. Don't abandon yourself because of grief; you are worthy of living a full and happy life. There is an unsung melody inside you waiting to be expressed. You haven't lost your ability to live fully or to enjoy life. It was natural that grief took you on a detour and it might even redirect your path, but be determined to stay engaged with life.

The eclipse of grief fades and the true you can then re-emerge. Finally there is a quickening of new life, a breakthrough, and then resurgence expands in your being. It can be a subtle transformation, but not always. Think of a plant pushing its way through a crack in cement. That plant had to do a lot to break through that hard surface, but it did what was necessary to get to the light. In your heart you are truly resilient. Eventually the rawness of your broken heart transcends to an expanded healed heart which is radiant and empowered. Your heart, having been stretched, is now capable of even more love, compassion, and passion than before. It has been forged in the fire of profound pain and proved its courage.

One night I fell asleep wondering what would be a good symbol of transcendence and transformation. I awoke in the night with the answer – a pearl. It is a perfect example of overcoming adversity by radiant transcendence. The oyster does not invite the grain of sand into its life just as we don't invite the pain of grief to enter our experience. The oyster embraces the particle of sand and with a slow process it works to soften the abrasive contours with layers of calcium, and a luminous pearl is created. We too have transformed our pain by taking the *Resilient Heart*® Journey.

By embracing and expressing our emotions and working with our thoughts we have softened the hard edges of our grief. We reconnected to the luminous qualities of our hearts and souls. With our *Resilient Hearts* we transcended our grief.

If you are reading these words and don't yet feel this transcendence, have faith in your inner resilience and hold fast to hope and determination as you continue your journey, knowing it is possible.

Say Yes to Life

I know it is a huge challenge to move forward in your life without your loved one by your side. It was for me, but finally it was time. I didn't want the fire to go out in my soul, so I embraced life again. I am reminded of this quote by Anais Nin, "And the day came when the risk to remain tight in a bud was more painful than the risk it took to blossom." I worked hard for nearly three years as I grieved as consciously as possible, but at fifty-four I felt I had a lot more life ahead of me. I now could see the "mourning" light after such piercing darkness.

Sometimes the things we can't change end up changing us. I couldn't change that Frank died yet I was definitely changed by his death. While I was grieving I spoke to a woman who had only known me since Frank died. She said I'd been blossoming during this short time. I explained that actually it was the real me resurfacing. With time I did transcend my old self. I became a victor of my grief, not a victim, and I finally experienced "mourning" glory. Ultimately I did feel like the Phoenix that rose from the ashes of my old life. **You too, can rise above your pain. Aim for flight!**

Have courage to be all that you are meant to be. The worst loss is what dies within yourself while you are alive. Brian, a friend, responded when asked if he was afraid of dying, "I am not afraid of dying; I am afraid of not truly living." Choose life and transcend the story of your loss: Don't let grief limit, contain, or define you. Your broken heart can become a blossoming one.

It is raining as I type these words, the first rain after a long, dry summer in Greece. Now the land will turn green and the wild flowers will burst forth from the soil. The storm will bring new life and rebirth after death. Your loved one died, but a wiser, stronger, more compassionate being can flower within you. There can be a return of vigor and purpose. Your suffering can bring a rebirth – your rebirth.

Life's circumstances at times force us to rebirth or re-craft a new life as well. Your future is coming whether you plan for it or not. I personally prefer not to be passive, but rather take some control where possible. Although some dreams and possibilities were lost, new ones can appear when you are open and alert. You have more gratifying, rich and purposeful experiences and growth waiting. By going towards life you aren't abandoning your loved one – they live in your heart forever and go with you. You are leaving the pain behind that you have processed.

Your spirit is calling you back into the game of life and wants you to live wholeheartedly. Are you answering that call? Your soul wants you to dare; to leap and stretch and ultimately to live outside the box of grief. Cherish your past, honor your loved one, and embrace your future. Be attentive to new directions or callings from within. Listen to your heart, as it knows the way.

Setting goals affirms we are open to life. Some desires are immediate and others take time and manifest in the future. There are more horizons for you to explore. If you have never set goals and don't know where to begin, you can get your copy of my *Your Ideal Life Assessment* available on my website GailSaunders. com. It will walk you through the different areas of your life with questions to consider when making new decisions. There are no right or wrong answers; it is about bringing awareness to make the right choices for you.

You can create a meaningful life despite your loss. In fact, sometimes it is your loss that inspires a meaningful life. Some transform their tragedy into a mission of hope or change. Often causes are championed because of loss. For example, parents have fought for greater measures of safety after the death of their child. MADD, Mothers Against Drunk Drivers, was created after an innocent child was killed by a drunk driver.

Genevieve Liu, a teenager in Chicago, focused her grief after the death of her father by creating a website to help other teens who lose a parent. Her website is called Surviving Life after a Parent Dies, SLAPD.com. The site has a forum for the teens to discuss their experiences of processing the death of their parent. There are interviews from experts and tribute pages with photos, poetry, and songs.

Many grievers have become committed to helping others in their time of bereavement by leading support groups or conducting speaking engagements. I am confident that if you feel moved to be of service because of the death of your loved one you will follow your inner guidance and do what best suits you.

As Frank was dying, he made me promise that I would do something to help others because of his death. By making this commitment to him he provided a lifeline to my future and I am publishing this book and offering an online *Resilient Heart*® *Grief* course. I have a second home in Greece, a perfect place to replenish and heal, that I make available for grievers and burnt out caregivers. Frank inspired my present life. **Our tragedies *can* become our triumphs.**

Doorways to Growth

Our wounds can become open doorways and portals to growth and transformation. What wisdom and insights have you gained from your experience with grief, your *Resilient Heart*® Journey? What have you learned along the way? Here are some things I compiled to share with a group about grief.

1. We are not alone, spiritually or physically. Strangers, friends, family and Spirit create a safety net and keep us from falling. We are all one!

2. Love doesn't die. Frank and his love continue. I still feel his presence in my life.

3. How right Frank and I were to live each day fully. I am determined to continue to do the same.

4. Prayers are answered, but not always in the way we imagine or sometimes desire.

5. The human spirit is invincible when we connect to our *Resilient Heart*®, our spark of the Divine.

6. There are gifts that appear through the gateway of pain: I feel stronger than ever before. I am working with death and dying. I've faced my worst fears and have had the courage not to be stopped in my tracks, but to work through my resistance. I've had some of my most profound spiritual experiences while grieving. I've learned to turn things over to God more often. I know how to ask for help which was a big growth for me. I have learned to say to another in need, "I want to support you through... How best can I help you?" I've learned how to care and love myself in a much grander style. I understand compassion in a deeper way.

Opening Your Heart to Another

At one point on your journey if you've lost your partner, your heart might open to the idea of allowing someone else into your heart space. I know if your loss is recent even reading these words might be repulsive. I remember feeling that way at my first support group gathering. Someone much further along on her grief journey shared over coffee how excited she was about going out on her first date since her husband's death. I could barely listen to her speak. If you are feeling that way now, just skip this section, but know it is here if and when you want to read more about re-entering the dating arena.

I had been forewarned that one is very vulnerable when first opening to the possibility of a new relationship. I found that to be very true. I might add to this that you should only venture forth when you are really ready. Someone I knew kept pushing for me to at least have coffee with a man she thought would be ideal for me. I continued to protest that I wasn't ready, but finally consented to meet him at a café. Things seemed fine until he asked me if I was romantic. I opened my mouth and said, "My late husband is more romantic in death than most men who are alive." I now know how to get rid of any man who I want out of my life! Let's just say it was a conversation and relationship stopper. I proved I wasn't ready to experience dating again at that time.

I wasn't ready for a long time. I met my first real date by chance at an airport. I hadn't had a date with someone besides Frank in thirty-one years. I won't go into the details, but I was quite vulnerable and I did get hurt. Yet on the positive side, I did learn that I could open my heart to another and that was a huge gift. So I keep my heart open, but to be cautious I proceed slowly. If you feel a desire to connect with someone, try not to judge yourself. It is life flowing through you and it is natural. I know how great life can be sharing it with the right person so I am now more open to the possibility of that happening again for me.

The Resilient Heart® Award

Each of us possesses extraordinary strengths, abilities, and possibilities. **We are capable of getting up and carrying on.** We each have an innate transcendent nature. You are resilient in the core of your being. Through your *Resilient Heart*® Journey you have been transforming your pain and ultimately you will transcend it. Your darkness has become a portal to the light of living. The weight has been lifted; you have freed your hijacked spirit. I would like to give you the equivalent to a Purple Heart for your courage to walk this path consciously, namely the *Resilient Heart*® Award.

In the crucible of grief, the supreme alchemist, our pain has become the source of growth and wisdom. We have mourned with soul: heart, depth, and attention. Through the alchemy of conscious mourning, harmony and grace can flow within and in our lives. We have transformed our pain into a luminous pearl.

Through this journey you have learned tools to respond to any future challenges that may come your way. I have just learned of the unexpected death of a dear friend and you too, might experience other deaths or other major losses. We don't become immune to death or loss but we now know:

- Our hearts are resilient
- Our grief doesn't have to define us
- Our wounds can lead to wisdom
- Trials do turn into triumphs

- Broken hearts can lead to a breakthrough
- Faith empowers
- Tragedy can become transformation
- Pain can become a mission of purpose
- Joy can transcend sorrow
- Hope opens doors
- Possibilities can become a new life

I wish to close by telling you what a precious honor it has been to walk with you on your *Resilient Heart*® Journey.

Heartfelt Suggestions

Now it is time to go to a quiet place where you can take some time for yourself. Bring a notebook and pen. Place your hand over your heart and close your eyes. Take several slow deep breaths down into your lower belly. Allow your breath to guide you to the peaceful place within your heart. Now open your eyes and begin reading and reflect on the suggestions. Remember this is part of your conscious mourning and it is sacred work.

1. Is anything still holding you back from venturing forward?

2. What have you learned through your grief journey?

3. Have you transformed your pain?

4. Are you open to a new chapter in your life?

5. Can you cherish your past, honor your loved one, and embrace your future?

MY NEXT CHAPTER

IT IS AN AUTUMN DAY HERE ON PAROS; the skies are filled with clouds, yet windows of blue are opening and streams of glorious sunlight are breaking through. I am watching my first fire of the season come to life in the fireplace. It is a soulful day for me, as it is Frank's birthday. I think it is the perfect day to write my "And Now What" piece to complete *Resilient Heart*®.

I'm not experiencing a riptide of emotions this year, but rather feeling a deep gratitude for the blessing it was to have had Frank in my life for the years we shared. I've processed my pain and now I am filled with deep peace. I want you to know how possible this gift is to claim. Writing this book, I reopened doors to my past that were recorded in my journals, which I've shared with you. I am moved to tears by how far I have traveled from the paralyzed Gail who was so desolate and lost in her early grief to the content and happy lady who sits here comfortably watching the fire flicker in her fireplace. I am humbled when I look back on the deep and soul wrenching *Resilient Heart*® Journey I personally walked. Of course, I still miss Frank's physical presence in my life, but his love continues to surround me.

My agonizing grief is now behind me. Fall is the season of harvest and celebration here in Greece. I just picked several pomegranates from my tree which I planted a couple years ago. Similarly, I have also sown new seeds in my life and have reclaimed myself. Let me share some of the seeds I planted and where I am now.

In the last chapter, I was heading for Africa. That turned out to be the right move for me, to have a totally different chapter in my life while in a foreign environment. The key is to figure out what you need and want after integrating the death of your loved one into your "new" life. There are no right answers or set rules to follow, but choose what is best for you and your family. Note that I thought of Africa as a chapter in my life. I think it would have been overwhelming to think of making the correct decision for the rest of my life during my time of grieving.

I wanted to reclaim my sense of adventure which is a big part of who I am. I didn't want to shrink my palette of possibilities due to fear and live smaller as a result. My years in Namibia at the Zebra River Lodge were just what I needed. I lived and worked with wonderful people. Every day new and interesting guests arrived from all points on the globe. I camped, hiked, and celebrated sun-downers in dramatic landscapes. I even had a near death experience with desert elephants that really gave me an extra dose of adventure! Africa was an amazing and wonderful experience for me – exactly what I needed!

After spending six years there I got definite nudges to move on. The lodge was for sale and work visas were getting more difficult to obtain. I opted to try to get a visa to move back to Greece to the island of Paros where Frank and I lived for ten years. I had our home there that I had kept as a rental property. I also had an unfinished project waiting for me. I wanted to finish the addition we had begun on the house seventeen years earlier. Before I knew I could obtain a visa, I took a risk and invested what money I had into completing the addition. Thankfully I did get my visa and moved into the extension. I continue to rent the original home to grievers, burnt out care-takers, writers, artists, and those just desiring time in a lovely sanctuary surrounded with sea views and a grove of olive trees. Once again I now have wonderful people coming to my doorstep.

Once I was resettled in my own beautiful home, I turned to the promise I made to Frank as he was dying; to help others deal with death and dying. While in Africa I transcribed my journal entries into my laptop. Of course, as you know, we don't grieve in an orderly fashion. My thoughts and emotions ricocheted in all directions on the pages. I began by sorting it all by subject which was an immense job, but not as huge as sorting them out in my psyche and life.

Fortunately my path crossed with Christine Kloser's desire to mentor writers to get their transformational books written and their messages out into the world. Her guidance has been invaluable in my own process. Through her I have also connected to a heart-based community of amazing authors whom are making incredible impact in the world. I have co-authored two books since living in Greece. One is entitled *Parian Chronicles: Foreign Affairs with a Greek Island* and the other has become a #1 International Bestseller in ten countries. It is called *Pebbles in the Pond (Wave Three): Transforming the World One Person at a Time.*

I have re-crafted my life several times. I've been a management consultant, artist/ instructor, masseuse, Reiki Master/Teacher, and coach. When attending university, I was torn whether to go the path of writing, journalism or speaking, and personal communications. At that time I chose the latter. Now at this point in my life I have circled back to writing, and all of my skills and areas of focus are brought together in a new and exciting kaleidoscope and a new vision has emerged.

I feel I can honestly say that this is one, if not the most, exciting times in my life. Intense passion and purpose fill my days as a transformational author and coach. It is so satisfying mentoring those in grief or those making a life transition, or guiding someone to experience greater joy in their life. I am now creating a Grieving Course to experience the *Resilient Heart*® Journey online. I also have a list of books that I am eager to write. The working title of one is *A Bridge to Everywhere: A Leap from Fear to Courage*. The richness I feel coming into alignment with my authentic mission is difficult to put into words... even for a writer! I am sure Frank is proud of me for carrying on with my life in typical Gail fashion, with exuberance as I walk through open gateways into my future.

Life is filled with changes: some are welcomed and some are not. I hope you can embrace your loss and integrate it with as much ease as possible into your life experience. Allow yourself to open new doors and write new chapters: see the wonder that life holds. Hold fast to your *Resilient Heart*®!

"A good half of the art of living is resilience." ~ Alain de Botton

CONTRIBUTORS & HONORED BELOVED ONES

Britta Ammitzboll, Nancy Baker, Victoria Rice Bean, Rosemary Robertson Bredeson, Ana Fatima Costa, Kaylan Daane, Janeann Dill, Lynn Finley, Chad and Anika Hammond, Velvet Hammond, Zemirah Jazwierska, Anita Johnson, Tamee Knox, Linda Kroll, Patricia Langdoc, Norie Marfil, Chris and Russ McIntyre, Jane Morris Pack, Susan Phelps, Clare and Martin Prentice, Lilia Shoshanna Rae, Elaine Santos, Julie Stamper, Ellen Webster Synakowski, Roseanne Tillotson, Briony Turner, and Pieter Verbeek thank you for your heartfelt contributions to the publishing of RESILIENT HEART.

Rosemary Bredeson remembers her beloved parents Kenneth and Gloria Robertson

Velvet Hammond lovingly honors the memory of her mom and dad, Miki and Cliff Stilwell

I too hold my wonderful parents Miki and Cliff Stilwell in my heart forever.

Anita Johnson wishes to honor her beloved mother, Mary Pashayan.

Linda Kroll honors Linda Wolfburg who is missed and loved by her family and friends

Julie Stamper honors the lives of her mother Connie S. Bunnell and her father-in-law Wallace W. Stamper

Ellen Synakowski wishes to honor her husband, Edmund Synakowski who has supported her in being her best self

Pieter Verbeek remembers his dear friend Nikos Raghousis

ABOUT THE AUTHOR

GAIL SAUNDERS IS A GLOBAL "Resilience Catalyst," life transition coach, mourning mentor, and a #1 International Bestselling transformational author. She transforms lives as she guides and empowers others to forge a full and rich life with meaning and joy no matter what their circumstance.

Gail has firsthand experience of transformation and resilience. On her own after her husband Frank died, for months she sat rocking back and forth engulfed in grief. She was $37,000 in debt, had to downsize from a large home to a small one-bedroom apartment, and take on responsibilities which she had no idea how to conquer. Yet she turned her life around going from broken to having breakthrough after breakthrough. Resiliently she changed her tragedy to triumph.

Now Gail's greatest joy is witnessing her clients and readers do the same as they step into their power and live wholeheartedly after any loss or major change in their life. It is her purpose and mission to ignite others to connect to their inner strength, wisdom, and wellspring of joy during times of challenge, loss, and transition, to be their guiding light, to give voice to expanded consciousness surrounding grief, joy, death, and life. In short, she becomes their "Resilience Catalyst."

Gail means "joy," and her zest for life is apparent in her daily actions and her laughter is infectious. She is a curious soul – an avid explorer of the unknown, and a world-traveling gypsy who always follows her heart. As a messenger and trailblazer she inspires her clients to also live fully with more happiness and gratitude.

Applying one's heart and soul is Gail's approach to everything. Her presence, compassion, comfort, wisdom, and joy permeate her life, her books, her coaching, and her speaking engagements. Gail is a captivating speaker and an engaging workshop facilitator who empowers and motivates the attendees. Believing the importance of seeing a greater perspective when out of one's normal life and landscape, Gail leads *Resilient Heart*® Soul Safari group workshops to Africa and Greece.

Having been on a trail of transformation while living in fifteen states and on three continents, Gail now resides on the gorgeous Greek Island of Paros with her one-eyed cat Romeo who is her writing muse. She can often be seen writing on her beach office by the sea. She also has a lovely home sanctuary which she rents for short or long term visits.

Gail's first degree is in education and she also holds a Master's of Science in education with a communications emphasis. She worked as a management consultant for the US Air Force, DuPont, Texas Instruments, and the Dallas Police Department, to name a few of her corporate clients. Gail specialized in stress management, corporate and personal goal setting, and interpersonal communication skills. The common thread of being an inspiring teacher has been interwoven throughout her career and life as well as being an avid learner. To connect with Gail go to GailSaunders.com.

ALSO BY GAIL SAUNDERS

Pebbles in the Pond: Transforming the World One Person at a Time
(Wave Three)
Parian Chronicles: Foreign Affairs with a Greek Island